# Advance Praise for *From Invi.*

"*From Invisible to Icon* is a must read for anyone who wants their brand to walk into the room long before they do. Through his captivating personal stories and practical advice, John Fareed unveils the secrets of crafting a personal brand identity that not only stands out but leaves an indelible mark on the minds of others."

—Kevin Short, Bestselling Author of *Sell Your Business for an Outrageous Price*

"John's book is an invaluable resource for anyone looking to enhance their personal brand. From the compelling quotes at the start of each chapter to the relatable personal stories and practical exercises that guide us in defining our unique path, this book is a treasure trove of wisdom. It's not just informative; it's engaging, insightful, and most importantly, actionable. Highly recommended for anyone on the journey of personal brand growth."

—David Kong, Founder and Principal of non-profit DEI Advisors and Former President and CEO of Best Western Hotels & Resorts

"*From Invisible to Icon* is a must-read for developing your personal and professional brand and achieving meaningful success in your industry. John Fareed's positivity is contagious, and his teachings are valuable and methodical, helping you unleash your brand's full potential."

—Laurent Halasz, Celebrity Chef, Entrepreneur, and Founder of Fig & Olive and Francine Restaurant

"After reading his book, it feels like I've known John Fareed forever! I am amazed at how many things he shared that just stuck with me. I constantly find myself using his principles

to promote myself as a real estate development expert. If you are looking for the 'how to' on creating a powerful, lasting and vibrant brand, *From Invisible to Icon* is for you."
—Steve Schroyer, Principal of Schroyer Resources

"*From Invisible to Icon* is a must-read for anyone desiring to achieve the next level professionally, personally or for the company they lead. A modern day, relatable success story and proven blueprint to guide your journey from what you do to 'who you are and how you do it.' If stepping out of the shadows and into the bright lights of center stage is for you, this book is a perfect guide."
—Randy Anderson, Cofounder and COO of Modexus LLC

"In this increasingly noisy and competitive business world, how do some experts become known as *the* superstar in their field? In *From Invisible to Icon*, John Fareed offers valuable insights and real-world steps you can take to differentiate and position yourself to be that person."
—Jim Burba, Producer, Cofounder Burba Hotel Network and Coauthor of *Smart Partners*

"Some people are born with a silver spoon. Some people attach themselves to others and 'inherit' that silver spoon. And then there are others like John Fareed who craft their own silver spoon. I've had the distinct pleasure and honor to work with John and consider him a master craftsman in that regard. Nothing but the utmost of respect and admiration for his work."
—Mark H. Brezinski, Serial Entrepreneur, Author, and One of Nation's Restaurant News' Top Influencers

"John Fareed knows personal branding. I took so many real ideas from his book that I kept saying 'yeah!' because they just made sense. The principles were easy to grasp and implement. I've already rolled many of his concepts into both my annual and long-term personal growth plans. I am ordering copies for friends."

—Matthew Kent, President and CEO
of Meteor Crater Enterprises

"Whether you're an aspiring entrepreneur, a seasoned professional, or simply someone looking to elevate their personal brand, this book is for you. John Fareed's expertise shines through, making *From Invisible to Icon* an invaluable resource."

—Mike Palmer, Managing Partner
at Ho'okipa Partners LLC

"*From Invisible to Icon*, which describes John Fareed's journey from small town Georgia to global hotel authority, is inspiring, entertaining and contains the wisdom and practical knowledge needed for anyone trying to make a name in any industry."

—Andrea Belfanti, CEO at International
Society of Hospitality Consultants

# FROM
## INVISIBLE TO
# ICON

### HOW TO BECOME A KNOWN
### EXPERT IN YOUR INDUSTRY

## JOHN FAREED
### WITH SEAN HUNTER

A POST HILL PRESS BOOK
ISBN: 979-8-88845-457-2
ISBN (eBook): 979-8-88845-458-9

From Invisible to Icon:
How to Become a Known Expert in Your Industry
© 2024 by John Fareed with Sean Hunter
All Rights Reserved

Cover design by Tom Macaluso
Cover photography by John Deeb

Although every effort has been made to ensure that the personal and professional advice present within this book is useful and appropriate, the author and publisher do not assume and hereby disclaim any liability to any person, business, or organization choosing to employ the guidance offered in this book.

No part of this book may be reproduced, stored in a retrieval system, or transmitted by any means without the written permission of the author and publisher.

Post Hill Press
New York • Nashville
posthillpress.com

Published in the United States of America
1 2 3 4 5 6 7 8 9 10

I dedicate this book to my *ride or die* partner and wife Lisa Fareed. Thank you for keeping me humble and grounded, while gently lifting me up and pushing me forward.

Just as in the first edition, I also dedicate this book to my son, J. Matson Fareed.
May your boots be always on the right feet, and the journey to *your* hero brand be one of magic and adventure.

# CONTENTS

# ACT III

# AUTHOR'S NOTE

This is a book about my life experiences, and the journey to *my* personal brand. It is based solely on my memories, which have their own story to tell, and I have done my best to make them tell a truthful story. The advice, examples and opinions I have shared—along with any inaccuracies—are solely my own, and are not meant to reflect negatively on any person, company or association. And for the record, this book features 100% human generated content.

# FOREWORD

## There is a lot of great stuff in here

*You will be the same person in five years as you are today
except for the people you meet and the books you read.*
—Charlie "Tremendous" Jones

L et's be honest for a moment. There are no shortcuts. No one way of achieving success. However, there are some universal principles that hold true for all of us and can make the difference.

To me, this book is like a mentor on the page. A mentor is a guide who leads you towards becoming the best version of yourself, refining the skills and techniques necessary for success.

The beauty of what John is sharing, the real diamond at the centre of his story, is the distillation of experience that takes away the noise and leaves you with the universal truths only someone who has encountered failures, and faced them repeatedly, can provide. John knows I mean that entirely as a compliment. As Niels Bohr said, "an expert is a person who has made all the possible mistakes you can make in a very narrow field."

While it's accurate to say that there's no singular path to success, it's equally valid that successful individuals share many common traits. If you fail to cultivate these traits, your chances of success are likely to remain limited.

The journey described in this book is unique to John and could not be replicated even if you tried. Too many variables, too many intangibles, chance meetings, lucky breaks and events that make for fantastic stories and anecdotes, all of which happened to John. In the hands of someone else, who knows what the outcome would have been? The point is to develop the tools to make your own story a success; to be yourself, only better.

What John's story shows is that it can take a long time, with several deviations along the way, to find your true passion and that's ok, in fact that's great. I am a firm believer in trying as many different jobs, in as many different industries as possible to find a place where you can thrive. Some people are born with a clear sense of what they will be doing right from the get-go. The rest of us need that trial and error to fully realise what we should be doing.

Where John's advice really comes to the forefront is when you have that realisation. What do you need to be doing to be a success? How can you take control of the narrative and make a plan for yourself, as opposed to seeing what happens and hoping for the best?

What I really took away from the book was John's positivity and optimism, two traits that don't receive the recognition they deserve. My advice, for what it's worth, read it. Start with the bits that you like and try them; there is a lot of great stuff in here. You are the star of your own movie, so start having what my daughter calls a *Main Character Moment*. What's the worst that could happen?

James Chappell, Global Business Director
Horwath HTL

# WELCOME TO THE REVISED AND EXPANDED EDITION

## This is not a *revised* edition

> *It is not the strongest species that survive, nor the*
> *most intelligent, but the most responsive to change.*
> —Charles Darwin

> *Never be defined by your past. It was only*
> *meant to be a lesson, not a life sentence.*
> —Mel Robbins

This is not a revised edition in the sense that the original is no longer relevant. There have been revisions over the last few printings—primarily corrections of typos and small mistakes—but this is the first revised and expanded edition.

The motivations for revisiting the book were simple. Things have changed dramatically since March 2013. Not just for me personally and professionally, but more importantly, for the world we live in today.

## Much has happened

Much has happened in the world since *From Invisible to Icon* was first published. Pope Benedict the XVI shocked the world by resigning as head of the Catholic Church—the first to do so since 1415. There was a widespread Ebola outbreak. The declaration of an ISIS Caliphate was followed by multiple terrorist attacks in France, Turkey, the Sinai, and the US. There were numerous mass shootings in the US from Orlando to Vegas, Parkland to Uvalde. There were elections of controversial leaders in the US and UK—and let's not forget Brexit. Social unrest from the #MeToo movement to Black Lives Matter and January 6th found its way to our front pages.

More recently, Russia invaded Ukraine, creating the largest conflict in Europe since World War II, and an armed conflict between Israel and Hamas-led Palestinian militants has just begun in the Gaza Strip.

On the lighter side, for the first time in 108 years the Chicago Cubs won the 2016 World Series. Prince Harry and Meghan Markle were married—breaking down centuries' old barriers of tradition, class, and race—before defecting from the Royal Family and moving to California. Same-sex marriage became legal in the US.

In January 2019, we saw the most diverse class of lawmakers in history sworn into the US Congress. The incoming class had a record-breaking number of women, people of color, and LGBTQ+ representatives—and among the 117 women newly elected to office, were the first Native-American woman and the first Muslim-American woman in Congress. My Muslim-born American mother would be proud.

The internet continued to reshape how we socialize, shop, view and experience media—do you still have cable television? Not to mention, it's fueled our ability to work from anywhere on the planet, creating the new global hybrid workforce and the seemingly unstoppable growth of *bleisure* travel—the combination of "business" and "leisure" travel.

And there is so much more, including Space-X and Blue Origin—billionaires in space, the evolution of EVs, and the unleashing of AI and ChatGPT. What's next?

## More Importantly

As I write this, in one way or another, the world is still recovering from the effects of the global pandemic. It changed almost everything about how we all live, work and yes, even love. No matter who you are or where you live, I'm certain that I don't have to explain this, as you lived through it. Either way, I feel safe saying the pandemic has forever changed our lives.

Much like the after-effects of 9/11, the pandemic negatively affected hotel, tourism and leisure—my industry—more than most others. More on this later, as I will share how the power of personal branding helped me push through the pandemic. Especially in comparison to my experiences after the events of 9/11, which was the impetus of my hero's journey, and subsequently the writing of *From Invisible to Icon*.

## And then, there's the *pivot*

Finally, I made a significant pivot since *From Invisible to Icon* was originally published. In the first edition, I shared about the growth and development of my personal brand as a solo practitioner under the John Fareed Hospitality Consulting brand.

In 2016, I opted to *level-up* my personal brand and join Horwath HTL, the world leader in hotel, tourism, and leisure consulting. The hundred-year-old firm boasts 250 senior consultants working out of sixty offices in more than fifty countries.

I am currently global chairman. I lead the global brand and oversee the firm's Americas offices.

The decision has changed everything for me professionally—and personally. I share the full story in the final chapter of the book, including my reasons for making the change and the impact it's had on my personal brand, my business and my future.

I hope that you enjoy the story, as well as the rest of this new revised and expanded edition, as much as I've enjoyed putting it together.

I also hope that you opt to harness the power of personal branding for *your* journey.

# PREFACE

## Where are you going?

> ... *the moment one definitely commits oneself, then Providence moves too. All sorts of things occur to help one that would never otherwise have occurred. A whole stream of events issues from the decision, raising in one's favor all manner of unforeseen incidents and meetings and material assistance, which no man could have dreamed would have come his way. Whatever you can do, or dream you can do, begin it. Boldness has genius, power, and magic in it. Begin it now.*
> —Someone other than Goethe

> *One's destination is never a place, but a new way of seeing things.*
> —Henry Miller

> *The key to realizing a dream is to focus not on success but on significance—and then even the small steps and little victories along your path will take on greater meaning.*
> —Oprah Winfrey

Stop. Right now. Where are you?

Maybe you're at home in bed curled up with a good book. Maybe you're at an airport, killing fifteen minutes before a connecting flight. Or even sipping a margarita poolside in Cancun. It doesn't matter. You're someplace on earth, the third planet from a mid-range star in the Milky Way galaxy, somewhere in the impossibly vast universe.

But where are you *really*?

You can't really measure your place in time and space alone. You're poised between success and mastery of your business. You're on the verge of closing the big deal. You're running the right path, on the way to meeting your goals, seizing your destiny.

Or maybe you have miles to go before you sleep…

And that's why this book is for you.

It's about going places. It's about positioning yourself as a known expert in whatever you do, and what it can mean for your brand.

In a way it's also about me, and my story. Years ago, I decided to leave a successful career as a professional magician, to become an expert in hotel marketing—and later hotel, tourism and leisure consulting—and it has indeed made all the difference. Along the way I learned a lot about how to position myself as a recognized industry expert, and I perfected a lot of techniques for achieving my goals. One thing I've learned is that…

## Personal branding isn't enough

It's true.

Sure, we all know that personal branding has become the secret weapon of today's business sphere. Just as the nature of business has been altered forever by the forces of branding, achieving success as an individual has also changed. In the same manner that most businesses fail to adapt and deploy effective brand strategies, most individual workers and professionals also fail to get it right.

Don't let yourself be one of them. The effects can be devastating. Whether facing challenging economies or growing global competition, it has become increasingly difficult to succeed using traditional means. It's no longer, "what have you done for me lately," it's, "what will you do for me tomorrow?"

On the other hand, if you position yourself as an industry expert, there's no limit to what you can do. It's that simple.

Look at media moguls Oprah or Martha Stewart, recording artists Lady Gaga or Taylor Swift, or chefs Nobuyuki "Nobu" Matsuhisa and Guy Fieri, or even astrophysicist Neil deGrasse Tyson. In my own industry you could look at Richard Branson of Virgin Hotels, or Ian Schrager, widely credited with creating the "boutique hotel" concept, or hospitality entrepreneur Chip Conley, best known as the founder of Joie de Vivre Hospitality, which grew to become the second largest boutique hotel chain in the US before being purchased by Hyatt Hotels. They all became wildly successful by creating a compelling personal brand, and then maintaining and expanding it consistently.

Sure, I suppose it's possible to be successful without perfecting your brand, but it's not easy. Being a genius would help. But even Einstein was a master of personal branding. Up until his recent biopic, not many could picture Robert Oppenheimer, but everyone could visualize Einstein. See what I mean?

For most of us, differentiation is everything. In today's world, you're either at the top or you're part of the faceless horde of mediocrity. We revere our superstars and reward them accordingly. In a typical company, what does the CEO earn versus next in command? What's the difference between #1 and #10 in a given industry? Let's be honest. No matter how good you are at what you do, if you don't find a way to stand out, you're facing a very tough future. More so now, in the post-pandemic economy, than ever.

## So think like an expert

Create a personal brand that allows you to maximize your ability to work at the top of your industry. A brand that gives you access to the right kind of publicity in the right places. A brand that brings customers and opportunities to *you*.

In the same way that personal branding can be broken down into key steps—assessment, analysis, application—positioning yourself as an expert comes down to knowing how to wield your personal brand in the right places and in the right ways.

If you select the right niche, and you understand where you are now and where you want to be in the future, then becoming a recognized expert is a natural extension of your long-term plan.

But thinking like an expert isn't enough. You also have to...

## Act like a hero

Why not? You're already the hero of your story. Why not become a hero in your niche?

The foundation of branding is essentially emotional. Beyond your calling cards, websites and social media channels, most personal brands come down to personal relationships and how people perceive you. In many ways, thinking of yourself as a hero is a nice encapsulation of the qualities of an expert. And who doesn't like a hero?

Heroes act in accordance with their values. Heroes solve key problems. Heroes are selfless.

Okay, we're going for a pure definition of hero here. No anti-heroes. Let's pretend post-modernism hasn't arrived.

But really you can define hero any way that makes sense to you. That's the beauty of it. What does a hero do? How does a hero act? What fires your imagination?

In his book *The Hero with a Thousand Faces*, Joseph Campbell talked about the fundamental links between all mythic heroes, and he described seventeen stages along a journey.

These seventeen stages can be divided into three parts: *Departure* (sometimes called *Separation*), *Initiation*, and *Return*. Departure deals with the hero venturing forth on the quest. Initiation deals with the hero's various adventures along the way. And Return deals with the hero's return home with knowledge and powers acquired on the journey.

While a lot of Campbell's analysis is not necessary for our purposes, the idea of the hero's journey is a great way to look at what it takes to position yourself as an expert. If you can't see yourself as a hero in your profession, then you may have bigger challenges than this book can solve.

In tomorrow's workscape, anything less than hero just isn't enough.

## This is for anyone

If you're in business for yourself, this book is for you. That's right – accountants, architects, attorneys, consultants, creatives, doctors, financial planners, insurance professionals, real estate professionals, and plumbers. And that goes for you corporate types as well. I'm sure you've figured out by now you're really working for yourself.

If you market your services, you need this book. These techniques are perfect for any small business owner or professional, whether you want to grow your brand internally or externally. It really depends on your business and personal goals. I know that not everyone is looking for global domination.

You just need to...

## Take the leap

In his book, *The Dip*, Seth Godin outlined the struggles we all go through as professionals, and how you have to know which battles are worth winning and which battles aren't. But he also talked about how valuable it was to get through the dip when it mattered most, and the spoils that await those who made it. *The Dip* had a lot to do with my decision to leave magic for hotel marketing.

If you're willing to go the extra mile, you can make a world of difference for yourself. That's why I'd say it's all about the leap. The jump to the top—the journey *from invisible to icon*. From benchwarmer to starter. From understudy to leading star.

But to get to where you want to go, you have to take the journey that every hero takes. Your vision quest. Your walkabout. It doesn't have to be in space or time, but it does have to be a step outside of your current place to a new one, a place where you are a recognized expert. A journey from where you *are* to where you want to *be*.

There are many stops along the way. There are skills and tools you will master. There are many twists and turns. But if you stay the course, you'll make it to your destination. Reach your destination, and customers and opportunities will come to you.

In this guidebook, I assume that you're already very good at what you do, an expert so to speak, and that you're now focused on lifting your industry profile. If so, keep reading. I'll show you how to position yourself as a *known* expert. How to use personal branding to greatest effect. How to become a resource for others. How to have all the answers, or even better, the right to decide what the answers are. How to anticipate and overcome the obstacles that lay between you and your place in the sun.

It's not magic, really. But the effects are truly magical. While I can't make you an expert, I can certainly help you along the way to becoming well recognized in your industry.

This is how I did it. This is how you can do it.

## You're ready now

It all begins with the call to adventure. Every hero makes a journey, but first they have to receive the call. They have to awaken to the possibilities. They have to feel the touch of destiny.

But you already knew that. That's why you're reading this book.

I'm asking you to know your story. I'm asking you to make your journey. I'm asking you to seize your destiny.

Are you ready to take the leap?

Are you ready to go from invisible to icon?

# ACT I

*A hero ventures forth from the world of the common day
into a region of supernatural wonder: fabulous forces
are there encountered and a decisive victory is won:
the hero comes back from this mysterious adventure
with the power to bestow boons on his fellow man.*
—Joseph Campbell

# 1

# MY STORY

## From Magic Boy to hotel marketing icon

*It's easy to decide what you're going to do. The hard
part is deciding what you're not going to do.*
—Michael Dell

*All journeys have secret destinations of
which the traveler is unaware.*
—Martin Buber

*Strangers on this road we are on,
We are not two, we are one.*
—The Kinks

From the beginning I knew I wasn't like other kids.
My Egyptian mother came to the United States on a
Rotary scholarship. In her first year at university, she fell
for a basketball star from Alabama. A young and naïve Muslim,
she was swiftly pregnant. She and my father quickly married,
but it was never healthy. He became a wandering schoolteacher who moved from school to school, and relationship

to relationship—while she played the role of the submissive, all-accepting housewife.

Her crushed father, my grandfather, was a devoted Muslim and self-proclaimed life planner. He had worked his way up from fighter pilot to Brigadier General in the Royal Air Force, then served as ambassador from the Arab League—currently composed of 22 member states—to Japan and eventually the United Nations. He finished his career in the hotel and travel industry by opening the Nile Hilton with Conrad Hilton—eventually running the company's Middle East division. He subsequently headed up Egypt Air Lines' public relations department until his retirement.

He was a self-made man with high ideals, who did exactly what most traditional Muslim men would do at the time, and more or less disowned my mother.

Sadly, mother was unable to finish college, never really worked, and for much of our lives together, relied on welfare and food stamps. If I never see another log of government cheese or box of powdered milk, it will be too soon.

My grandfather had two daughters. I was the first-born male within the Fareed family. In order to build and maintain a relationship with me, he would send round-trip tickets to Egypt each summer, where I lived like a virtual pharaonic king. I enjoyed estates with servants, bespoke clothes, and all the food I could eat—albeit lamb, tabouleh and stuffed grape leaves.

The two diametric lifestyles made me a bit of a misfit.

At the beginning of every school year, when my small-town Georgia classmates stood up in front of the class and talked about fishing, visiting theme parks and building forts all summer vacation, I nervously related my adventures riding camels, climbing pyramids and playing on Egyptian beaches.

4

Sigh. I longed to just be a normal American kid.

At the time I didn't really enjoy those exotic summer excursions either, as I felt our well-heeled relatives and family friends looked down on my mother and me. It wasn't easy.

Although I didn't realize it at the time, the travel proved to be an amazing educator. It was in Egypt that I had my first taste of entrepreneurship. We usually spent half our summer in Cairo and the other in Alexandria, where we had a beach cottage on the grounds of the Montaza Palace. It included the original Salamek Palace built in 1892 and renovated as an official presidential residence by then President Anwar El-Sadat. It was a truly magical place for a young boy to summer.

It was there I started my very first *business enterprise*, collecting sea urchins—cleaning and preparing trays full of them. I sold them to fellow cottagers for Egyptian pounds so I could buy sweets at Maison Groppi's, a famed bakery, chocolatier and tea shop located on the first floor of the palace.

The experience taught me lifelong lessons about packaging, demand and revenue management. I learned that an attractive tray with fresh lime slices and a pretty seashell sold best, that late afternoon was the highest demand period, and if a customer smiled too big when I quoted them my price, I needed to ask for more next time.

I also had another life-changing experience in Alexandria.

During one Egyptian summer, when I was ten, I saw a street magician who made daily stops at the beach cottages. The performer was known as the Hully-Gully Man, the Arabic name for a magician. He did all kinds of cool things. He did the old cups-and-balls trick with colorfully dyed baby chicks. He formed strips of fabric into a ball, lit them on fire, placed them in his mouth and pulled them out again—all tied together! Like many kids at that age, I thought I knew everything, but this guy did tricks that…

## Mesmerized me

When I returned to Georgia that fall, I ransacked the library for books on magic. I checked out the only one I found, a 1930s magic tome called *Greater Magic* by John Northern Hilliard, that was so out-of-date that many of the ingredients I needed for tricks were no longer available. I kept that book checked out perpetually, checking it out again and again. Eventually, the town librarian ordered more books on magic for me. Those books fired my growing passion. Before long, I was obsessed with sleight of hand, tricks of the mind, and the incredible power of the imagination.

I'd finally found a place where I fit in. Like many before me, magic was a way for me to gain respect. None of my friends could perform such feats, and they had no idea how I did them.

I devoured every book and trade magazine I could find on the subject. I signed up for the mail-order *Mark Wilson's Course on Magic*, purchased with my hard-earned lawn-mowing money. By the time I was eleven, I was performing at birthday parties, for the local men's and women's clubs, and in area festivals like the annual *Georgia Apple Festival* in my hometown of Ellijay— wherever I could get a booking.

I began to dream of a life spent traveling the world in elegant style, performing magic. I was naïve enough to be completely unaware that magic's vaudevillian heyday had passed. But then I faced the challenges that we all face. The choice between our dreams and what is practical.

Then there was my conservative family, who never really supported my passion for magic. My senior year of high school, my grandfather, the retired Egyptian general and former ambassador, laid down the law. There would be no hully-gully for his grandson. I would join the military, as was customary for all men in the Fareed family. I argued, but my grandfather explained the consequences. He would disown me.

Clearly, I got his message. But I thought for a moment and said, "Grandpa, you've taught me much about life—how a gentleman buys clothes, folds a handkerchief, uses proper table manners and most importantly, negotiates. You're demanding much of me, and I should ask for something in return." He stared back at me without word or expression as I continued, "I'll join the military, if you'll take my mother back—fully."

I watched nervously as he slammed his hand on the table, pushed his chair away and stepped out on the balcony. I thought it was early in the day for him to have a whiskey and a cigarette, but apparently it wasn't. I began to panic.

The general returned to the table, sat down and stared at me for nearly twenty minutes. He had taught me that when negotiating, once you make your ask, the first one to speak loses. The room was eerily quiet. "Agreed!" he said sternly, "But it has to be the US Marine Corps." I was devastated, but I did my grandfather's bidding. He and my mother remained close for the rest of their lives. Looking back, it was totally worth it—my grandfather and my granny Lulu later moved to North Georgia to be closer to the family.

As it turns out the Marines understood a bit about show business. The Marine recruiter drove a DeLorean, and dressed as though he were in a theatrical production—think Dress Blues. Even as a Marine I continued to dabble in magic. I opted for the Marine reserves, which allowed me to travel and perform in clubs and at special events. I served six years and eventually received an honorable discharge.

## Persistence is a virtue

But I still couldn't shake the magic bug, and chose to take a chance on Hollywood. One impulsive Saturday morning, I left on an Amtrak train with less than $100 in my pocket. Luckily, the train stopped for an overnight in New Orleans, and I earned enough money performing on the streets of the French Quarter to get to Los Angeles—more on that later.

A few lucky breaks later, I found myself performing at Hollywood's legendary Magic Castle. That led to a job with TV magician Mark Wilson, my magic idol, working as assistant producer on a show that toured the country.

But it wasn't enough for me. The production job meant setting someone else up to do the tricks and I wanted to be the *hero*—the guy up on stage doing those tricks. I wanted to be the star of the show.

I quit the job, headed back to Georgia and began performing in clubs and bars. It paid, but not very much. I always had to do something else to get by. I began a string of jobs, from a stint as the local mall marketing director to selling everything from fiber optics to advertising. Through it all magic continued to call to me. Whenever something would come along in my jobs to advance my career, I'd give it up for the magic. I was always talking about doing it full time, and I continued to dream of a magical lifestyle.

## Along the way I learned a lot

Why is all of this important? It was during my career as a magician that I first learned the power of personal branding.

I knew that to be successful, I had to find a way to stand out from all the other magicians out there. I had to find a niche. I had to find a way to be remembered.

So, I went to work. I joined local organizations for magicians, which in turn connected me to national organizations. I started writing for the trades—*The Magic Menu, The Illusionist, Marketing Magic*—and even became a contributing editor for *Magic* magazine, the industry's bible. It did work magic for my career at the time, as I built status and reputation. It gave me entry.

In my 15-year career as *Magic Boy*, I played everything from cruise ships to Las Vegas casinos to the famed Magic Castle in Hollywood, traveling *Around the World in 80 Tricks*.

## Then I had a realization

As I sat amid the shelves of magic books and props, classic magic posters and photographs, and scattered memorabilia that filled my magic room, I realized that no matter how accomplished I became as a magician, there would always be serious limitations to what I could do. I realized my career as a magician was at least a cul-de-sac, if not dead-end.

You see, magic is just like any other industry. The people at the very top make exorbitant amounts of money, while the typical magician toils in relative obscurity. Sure, I could work a little harder, a little smarter than the others and carve a niche for myself. But in the end the industry was so small and limited, that the odds of achieving the kind of success I was looking for were relatively low, no matter how hard I worked.

I realized that even more important than my success as a magician, were the methods I used to become successful. What if I applied that same effort and intelligence in a different field where there was a much bigger pie from which to grab a piece?

If I was going to persevere through the fight to the top of my industry, was this what I wanted most? Was this worth it? I decided to make a change.

## Welcome to hotel marketing

At first, I was quite successful at my journey into hotel marketing. I employed a lot of the techniques that had made me successful as a magician. As always, I read everything I could. I joined all the organizations I could. I wrote for the trades. I made a name for myself, just as I had in magic.

But there were a lot of things I didn't know. There was a vicious process of trial and error. My firm was essentially a bootstrap organization, and we learned as we went along. We were successful for the most part, but I still hadn't turned the corner to achieve the kind of success I sought. I quickly reached a limit in my hotel marketing business and realized I had found another cul-de-sac. What was I doing wrong?

I soon discovered that the industry did not value marketers nearly as much as highly educated, experienced industry consultants—*experts*.

I remember being at a conference cocktail party one night, looking around at the power players in the industry. I realized that in many cases they received business just for being who they were. People actually came to them, instead of them having to actively seek clients. They received the most select, highest-paying opportunities not because of what they did, but because of who they were. Or rather, *where* they were. They had positioned themselves as successful industry experts.

I realized that rather than continuing to try to win every battle in the hotel marketing arena I could, I needed to position myself as a recognized *full-service* industry expert. I needed a way to open those closed doors rather than breaking them down. I had to go back to zero again so that I could rebuild in the right way.

Then 9/11 happened. The ensuing economic crisis effectively put an end to my seven-year-old hotel marketing firm. Today, as I look back on it, the fallout from this horrific tragedy was a huge part of what helped me succeed.

I started from scratch. I went back to zero.

## A new plan

The need to shutter my hotel marketing business—post 9/11— gave me a chance to go after the right skills, the right credentials, the right education to make my plan work. I decided to become a recognized full-service consultant in the hotel, tourism and leisure industries. I focused on work that would build credentials, experience and knowledge, rather than just a series of checks.

I put together a five-year plan to become a genuine expert in my field—the plan that has brought me to where I am today. I went to work at a large historic resort, living in the staff dorms. I perfected my skills in speaking, writing, and developing workshops. I garnered keynote gigs at major industry events around the globe. I resolved to find the most prominent industry experts I knew and work with them on key assignments—on a contract basis of course. I earned or won all of the relevant industry credentials possible.

Then the only milestone that remained was my goal to further my education. I had a very tough choice to make, because I finally had a successful career underway in the right places. But I still needed to get an advanced degree, ideally in a strong hotel management graduate program. A lot of my friends and colleagues thought going back to school at that time seemed crazy. Not to mention I was in my early forties. How could I leave all income, prestige and security behind? But I could go no further until I took...

## A leap of faith

Actually, I took an airplane from the US to Ireland. I stepped away from a substantial income, and out of the marketplace, to go back to school at the Dublin Institute of Technology's, currently Technological University Dublin, School of Hospitality and Tourism Management. I traveled halfway around the world to begin a new act in my life.

Why?

I had to move toward my goal—to position myself as a highly educated, experienced industry consultant. I knew that everything else was just spinning my wheels.

Was I nervous? No. I knew where I'd land. Even though it was a huge risk, it was easy. I had a plan that took me from moderately successful magician to a recognized expert in my new field of choice—hotel, tourism and leisure.

I planned the trip for a year, saving the necessary monies to sustain me at school. The day I left, I was in my oldest clothes, with a suitcase filled with all the new clothes, shoes and accessories I'd been collecting for months to signify my new personal *grad student* brand.

At 30,000 feet above the Atlantic, I had a lot of time to think. It was a strange experience because I had no work to do on the plane. I was truly transitioning from one life to another. I was untethered. It was one of those rare moments in life where you can reflect on where you've been and where you're going. Traveling does that to you.

When my plane set down it was 6am in Dublin. My long-standing industry friend and colleague, Alex Gibson, picked me up at the airport and we went to breakfast. As the sun rose over the beautiful Irish landscape, a new day dawned for me as well.

## And then what?

Today I'm happy to report that I hold two postgraduates including a Master of Science degree from the Dublin Institute of Technology's School of Hospitality Management and Tourism (currently Technological University) in Dublin, Ireland, as well as a Hotel Real Estate Investments and Asset Management Certificate from Cornell University.

I possess professional designations from the prestigious International Society of Hospitality Consultants (ISHC) and the Hospitality Sales and Marketing Association International (HSMAI). HSMAI recognized me as one of the "Top 25 Extraordinary Minds in Sales and Marketing." I am Global Chair Emeritus of both ISHC and the Board of Trustees for HSMAI's International Foundation.

I speak regularly at industry conferences and events around the globe, and have spoken on hotel, tourism and leisure related topics in Australia, Brazil, Croatia, Egypt, France, Germany, Hungary, Ireland, Italy, Mexico, Oman, United Kingdom, and across the US, Canada and Caribbean.

My client list includes Fortune 500 companies, global brands, lenders, developers, REITs, management companies, investors, owners, attorneys, and insurers. I've also provided expert witness and litigation support in a number of major cases relating to lodging real estate investment issues.

I'm often quoted as an industry expert—my goal all along—and I've appeared on national programs including ABC News, CNN and Fox News Network, in national publications such as *USA Today*, *The New York Times*, and *The Washington Post*, and have had many articles published in trade journals.

I've lectured at some of the world's best hotel schools including Cornell University's School of Hotel Administration in Ithaca, New York, and the Institut de Management Hôtelier International (IMHI) at the École Supérieure des Sciences Economíques et Commerciales (ESSEC), one of Europe's pre-eminent business schools, in Paris, France.

And as I shared earlier, for the past several years I have been global chairman of Horwath HTL. More on this *pivot* later.

In short, today I am an internationally recognized industry leader and a highly regarded, known expert.

I have to say that writing all this down, made me feel pretty damn good about myself. It's been a great ride so far.

But this book is about you, and what you can achieve.

I did it. You can do it. You just need the right roadmap to make your journey.

# 2
CHAPTER

# PERSONAL BRANDING: WHY

## It was the best of times

*By now even the dimmest observers recognize that
the United States and numerous other countries are
transitioning to brain-driven "knowledge economies."
But the full impact of this change—on individuals and
on whole countries and continents—has yet to be felt.
The past half-century has merely been prologue.*
—Alvin Toffler, *Revolutionary Wealth*

*The attention economy is a star system...If there is
nothing very special about your work, no matter how
hard you apply yourself you won't get noticed, and that
increasingly means you won't get paid much either.*
—Michael Goldhaber, *Wired* (Taken from *BrandYou 50*)

*A traveler without observation is a bird without wings.*
—Moslih Eddin Saadi

*Brand is the "f" word of marketing. People swear by it,
no one quite understands its significance and everybody
would like to think they do it more often than they do.*
—Mark di Soma, Audacity Group

15

Once upon a time everyone thought the sun revolved around the earth, the earth was flat, and man would never travel faster than the speed of sound.

Just as once it was all about what you did, what company you worked for, and where you were perched on the corporate ladder.

Oh, how things change.

Revolutionary forces are afoot, from paradigm-shifting technology to accelerating globalization to innovative work processes and heightened connectivity. Tomorrow's workspace will continue to evolve rapidly—think "gig economy"—and will in no way resemble what many professionals are accustomed to. Or comfortable with.

It happened when the industrial revolution was born. It happened when the cotton gin was invented. It happened when the computer landed on our desktops. It happened when that same computer shrunk down to fit in our hands, and linked to others like it everywhere. From the farms to the factories to the docks, the time it took for workers to perform a host of menial tasks was slashed.

The service industry was next, as technology changed the way companies interacted with consumers in myriad ways. New standards and practices were established, and new possibilities emerged.

But the past is only prologue. Now it's happening to knowledge workers. Most of us in white collar jobs haven't worried about similar changes affecting what we do. But now everything's different. To quote Tom Peters, "The White Collar Revolution is on."

Sure, your profession won't change overnight, but it will be totally redefined. As the world continues to change at an accelerating pace, our chosen professions will come under the same productivity pressures that manufacturing has faced. Everything we do will be under more scrutiny. Our connectivity will increase at a sharper curve, currently demonstrated by the post pandemic "hybrid"—in-office, remote, and on-the-go—work environment in which we live. Anyone else tired of virtual meetings?

The forces at work range from new information technology to innovative enterprise resource planning systems to virtual customer management. Increasing globalization is creating competition in all fields. Witness the reshaping of corporate culture, and the growing shift to processes that require ad hoc teams—often independent contractors—for projects.

What changes are next?

There will be new rules, new challenges, and yes, new opportunities. The work-reinvention revolution is a shining new opportunity for freedom and inspiration—in our professions and in our personal lives.

Why not embrace it?

In the late 1800s everything changed when the first transcontinental trains ran and suddenly made it possible for people to travel around the world, anywhere they wanted. Now you can go anywhere professionally. You are not bound by the constraints of yesterday—your company, your title, your hometown.

But how do you take advantage of this different universe? How do you seize the day?

You must change with it. Regardless of your age or background, you must adapt to the times. In a knowledge-based economy, it's vital to your perceived value in the marketplace to establish yourself as a true professional and a recognized expert in your field. You have to be "THE" person.

You have to…

## Master the power of personal branding

You need to differentiate. You need to stand out. You need to become a throwback to a different time, when you were only as good as your name. Become a self-reliant, brilliantly networked, word-of-mouth maestro. A super-powered problem solver. A professional hero.

We've all heard the phrase *personal branding*. My first exposure to the concept came in the form of a brilliant article titled "The Brand Called You" by Tom J. Peters published in *Fast Company* magazine in August 1997. In it, Peters posits, "Regardless of age, regardless of position, regardless of the business we happen to be in, all of us need to understand the importance of branding. We are C.E.O.s of our own companies: Me Inc. To be in business today, our most important job is to be head marketer for the brand called You." In short, he urges us to cement our professional reputations by developing our own brands.

It literally changed my life. Though Peters didn't use the term personal branding, defining the concept as "Brand You = Who You Are," but his general theory was groundbreaking and remains consistent with how we perceive the concept of image management today.

But what makes personal branding more than just another catchphrase in the business sphere? Why is it so important to have a proactively defined identity now?

There are as many different definitions of personal branding as there are practitioners.

It's the development and management of your personal presentation. Curating your public personal so to speak. It's about painting a vivid self-portrait in the minds of the people in your life—family, friends, colleagues, customers and prospects. One that conjures up precise and meaningful thoughts about your gifts, beliefs, values and what you do for a living.

Start with branding 101. Everyone knows what it is, right? But everyone has a different way of looking at it. Marketing guru

Al Ries said, "What's a brand? A singular idea or concept that you own inside the mind of a prospect." Michael Eisner said, "A brand is a living entity—and it is enriched or undermined cumulatively over time, the product of a thousand small gestures."

I would say a brand reflects the relationship an organization has with its customers—internally and externally. It's a relationship that involves the kind of trust that only happens when value systems of product and consumer line up. Brand is a familiar bridge across which businesses and their customers conduct transactions that lead to long-term and mutually beneficial relationships.

It's not a clever tagline, or a colorful image, or an artificial creation disguising the true nature of what's within. A brand *reveals* what's best about a product or company.

It is a "trust" mark, but it's also a sorting device. As *Brandweek* put it, "Brands are the express checkout for people living their lives at increasing speed." As our lives accelerate and our bandwidth is strained, we filter using them as shorthand. This has never been truer than it is today.

Personal branding, on the other hand is, well, a lot more *personal*. It takes all the characteristics of branding and applies them to your professional identity. As author and speaker Peter Montoya put it, a personal brand is "a personal identity that stimulates a meaningful emotional response in another person or audience about the qualities or values for which a person stands."

In short, personal branding is the art of defining *yourself* to your audiences in the right way.

## Exempli gratia

It's not hard to find examples of powerful personal brands. Our culture is dominated by them.

Oprah Gail Winfrey leveraged hers, *Oprah*, to become the host of the highest-rated talk show in the history of television, an Oscar and Emmy winning actress, the richest and most philanthropic African American in history, and one of the most influential women in the world.

And she did it all through the power of her signature personality, character and reputation.

How would you sum up her brand in three or four words? I'll go with intelligent, compassionate, sincere, and influential. She is most certainly a mogul.

And I'll wager your words were not too different than mine. That's the power of a personal brand. You know clearly what she stands for. The essence of what she represents is evident, and the manner with which she has conducted herself in the face of such resounding success has only further strengthened her image.

But examples of great personal brands are everywhere.

Madonna Louise Ciccone turned her personal brand into one of the greatest pop acts of all time. Considered by many the worlds' most successful female recording artist. She's a seven-time Grammy winner, two-time Golden Globe winner, and a Rock and Roll Hall of Fame inductee. When I mention Madonna, you know she's an outrageous and sexy chameleon, who seems to defy the stereotypes regarding aging women. Her brand is so strong that even hit maker and actress Lady Gaga lives in Madonna's shadow, often referred to as "the new Madonna."

Martha Stewart turned her personal brand into great success, as former television host of *Martha*—broadcast throughout the world, bestselling author, and publisher of *Martha Stewart Living* magazine. More recently appearing in national broadcast commercials with Snoop Dogg and as cover model of the 2023

Sports Illustrated Swimsuit issue—at the age of 81. When I say Martha Stewart, you may think organized, creative, strong, and perhaps even bossy or intimidating at times.

Richard Branson, best known for his Virgin brand of over 400 companies—including Virgin Galactic, is one of the richest people in the world, thanks to his memorable brand. Richard Branson has proven himself to be adventurous, flamboyant, energetic, and passionate.

Sure, these are big name celebrities. But you can pick out people in your own industry who have distinguishing personal brands already. In my industry, you can look at someone like Jonathan M. Tisch, Chairman and CEO of Loews Hotels, best-selling author and media personality, who gave an endowed gift of $40 million dollars to fund the Jonathan M. Tisch College of Citizenship and Public Service. Jonathan Tisch is community-focused, generous, reserved, and approachable.

John Willard "Bill" Marriott Jr., who's conservative, distinguished, spiritual, and a global leader—is another example of a clearly defined *icon* brand within the hotel industry.

Now, let's get to work. What four words would people use to describe you? More importantly, what four words would you *like* them to use?

## What's in it for you?

A great personal brand can help you succeed in an increasingly competitive and complex business world.

It will help differentiate you from your competition, let your customers know what to expect, tell your story, and hone and project your key values. It will help you achieve the emotional connection that will make you a hero in the eyes of your clients.

When leveraged correctly, a strong personal brand will help you position yourself as an expert.

Look at it this way: your personal brand is an umbrella of all the qualities you need to possess in order to succeed.

A great personal brand separates you from the sea of sameness and helps you to thrive. It helps people know what to expect. As you reinforce it consistently, it will cause people to respond to you just as you'd like them to, so when they hear your name they conjure positive associations.

A great personal brand helps you tell your story, carrying the key messages for you. Professionals with great identity management don't have to go around telling everyone what they're about. They are *known*.

A great personal brand will help you define and reinforce your values, becoming the embodiment of what you value. It transforms into a self-fulfilling cycle. Your brand is how you act; you act as your brand.

Finally, a great personal brand will help you forge an emotional connection. It taps into emotions, and emotions drive our decisions. In the relationships that matter in your life, the heart rules. Decisions are often affected by intangible, as opposed to measurable, variables. A great brand reaches out on an emotional level as a powerful connecting experience that transcends the product or service.

In a perfect world, we are guided by our objective thoughts. But more often than not we are affected in subtle ways by our emotions. The heart defies the head, and we cling to feelings, positive or negative, that defy rational analysis. That's what makes us humans.

## Enter the icon brand

If a brand is a relationship and a personal brand is a personal relationship, then an *icon brand* is a personal relationship that maximizes that emotional connectivity. The higher you are on the pyramid, the stronger the emotional connectivity.

**Meaningful Emotional Connection**

But no matter what your vision of life may be, the most critical component of your ultimate success is the breadth and depth of your relationships. Your icon brand will help you forge the connections you need to get where you want to go.

Beyond the generalities, it is the icon brand that will help you get published. It will help you get invited to speak. It will help you get calls out of the blue from make-me-famous clients.

## You already have a personal brand

It's true. Whether you realize it or not, your family, friends, colleagues and clients already have some definite ideas about your personal brand. How do you think they would describe your personal brand if asked?

Nervous?

You have to brand yourself before someone else does it for you—or to you—or change your brand if it doesn't reflect your true self.

Why not make it an icon brand?

Why not position yourself as an expert and be seen as the very best, the most emblematic solution for your target niche.

## Get going

The spoils await. Set out on a quest to become your most bona fide professional self.

Your challenge is to create a brand that's a vehicle for your most authentic self. In this way you'll distinguish yourself from others who do similar work, affirm your true identity, highlight your talents, and re-establish your professional reputation.

If you make the journey to known expert, you'll be better positioned within your industry. You'll never have a problem getting a job. You'll earn significantly more money, and work in better environments. Your work will be much richer, varied and rewarding.

By developing a strong personal brand that is clear, complete, and valuable to others, you will create a life that is much more successful and fulfilling. You win. They win. That's the kind of success that can have far-reaching benefits.

Like anything else, it comes down to small steps. Take the important first step.

Let's go!

# 3

CHAPTER

# *PERSONAL BRANDING: HOW*

## Awaken your icon brand

> *The unexamined life is not worth living.*
> —Socrates/Plato

> *Carpenters bend wood. Fletchers bend
> arrows. Wise men fashion themselves.*
> —Buddha

> *Branding demands commitment; commitment to continual
> re-invention; striking chords with people to stir their
> emotions; and commitment to imagination. It is easy to be
> cynical about such things, much harder to be successful.*
> —Sir Richard Branson

Mastery of personal branding is a critical part of your mission.

It helps you clearly define, express, and convey who you are, what you do, and why you have chosen to devote your energy to serving your target market. It enables you to attract your dream clients, those who understand and *get* you, and to distance yourself from those who don't.

Your personal brand is a lot more than just what you do and how amazingly well you do it. It is the essence of who you are. It is the entire dynamic of your thoughts and actions, your past and future.

To achieve its greatest power, it needs to be clear, consistent, authentic, memorable, and meaningful. It needs to signify at a glance how you are unique compared to everyone else in your niche.

Seize your brand. The process focuses on four key areas: your key attributes, your packaging, your description and your mission statement. You'll need to realistically assess where your personal brand is currently and then determine where you want to take it. You'll need to...

## Discover your key attributes

Yes, your personal brand is a reflection of you. But first you have to reflect on *it*.

Let's break it down into a two-part process. The first part is about who *you* are. The second part is about how that fits into your internal and external *customers'* needs.

Ultimately, your goal is to come up with four words to describe you. Piece of cake, right?

Ask yourself a series of questions. How are you unique— *truly?* What are your most memorable personal traits? What do you *really* do? It's certainly more than the job title or description you were last assigned. What are the attributes that most distinguish you from your colleagues and competitors? When tapped for a project or assignment, what do you bring to the table that adds genuine, measurable value at the end of the day?

Dig deep and keep on digging. It takes a lot of personal excavation to unearth that hidden quirk or natural talent that's been waiting to bring you wealth, happiness, and unbridled success in your business. What are your special talents? What have you been good at since you were a kid? What do people compliment you on? What do you have a passion for in your personal life? Many times, it's those qualities that make you uniquely you—qualities that come so naturally, you don't even think about them—that become the best aspects of your personal brand.

Then go to your family, friends and colleagues. Reach out to at least five people in your life, preferably from different areas, and ask them to identify your top five personality traits or quirks. Ask for memorable experiences they've had with you. Essentially, ask them to describe you and your personal brand, and encourage them to be bold and tell the unvarnished truth. I know this isn't easy, but you need to do it! There is treasure here, but you won't discover it if you don't dig.

What do *they* say?

Now on to your clients.

- What would your customers say is your greatest and clearest strength?
- Why do they work with you?
- What do you do for them?
- What do you offer beyond your basic services?
- What intangibles do you offer?
- Where is your expertise most valued?
- What fires have you recently put out or challenges have you helped them solve?

In consumer branding, every feature of a product or service yields a distinct and identifiable benefit for the customer. For instance, an important part of the Ritz-Carlton brand is the personalized service it lavishes on each and every guest. The benefit is a feeling of being accorded individualized attention—along with all the delightful amenities of a world-class hotel or resort.

What is the big feature-benefit for your personal brand? Both feature and benefit are an important part of selecting your key attributes.

Do you save your clients money? Every client faces budget overruns. Do you have a particular ability to think strategically, globally—or both, to solve problems or create solutions across departments? Integration is always a challenge, and an opportunity. Do you foresee problems and solve them proactively? Do your customers save money and headache just by having you around?

Another way to think about it is in terms of problems, solutions and results. You begin with your customers' concerns. What major problems do they face? What is the solution that you offer? What is the end result, the pay-off for them, beyond just solving the immediate problem?

When you can solve specific problems for clients, it creates more emotional resonance for your personal brand. The greatest triumphs in your business will come when you find out exactly what your clients need on a deep personal level. Don't just look at the surface of problems. Find out what they're *really* looking for. What is the deeper problem? What do they really want? What results do they want to achieve? How will their life be intrinsically better once they start working with you? How can you make your clients look like superstars to the people they answer to? How can you connect with them emotionally and leave them feeling better for having spent time with you?

That's how you become an iconic brand.

So, think about the biggest challenges in your industry, in your niche.

For instance, in the lodging real estate investment industry, a client may have an underperforming asset and is in need of an expert to reposition the property for greater returns. An owner may need a savvy representative, or asset manager, to ensure their hotel is consistently being operated to its greatest potential—maximizing profitability—by the third-party management company, in an effort to increase the value of the hotel real estate. Or a hotel franchise company may be looking for assistance with crafting a global brand strategy designed to significantly grow their properties—via franchise licenses and management contracts—around the world.

Apply this formula to your industry and then look at what you offer that meets their greatest challenges. Are any of your key attributes a part of those solutions?

Now it's time to choose three to four words that are really "you." Words you hope will one day be used by others to describe you. Four words that come together to answer the question: "What makes you an icon?"

Do it. Do it *now*. In the margins of this book if you need to. It's a start.

For example, the four words that I use to describe my personal brand are:

*Creative—Visionary—Knowledgeable—Genuine*

I chose the word *creative* because it is a core personality trait. In everything I do, I try to be as creative as possible. I strive for imaginative and successful ideas and solutions for both my team and our clients.

I chose the word *visionary* because it captures both my ability to see the big picture and to anticipate future developments. In the rapidly evolving hotel, tourism and leisure field, my clients require the ability to adjust to changes and take advantage of new opportunities—and my team has to be well equipped and ready to assist them.

I chose the word *knowledgeable* because it is a foundational character trait of mine. I read constantly, and I'm a perpetual student. If I don't know the answer, I will find it. As we all know, knowledge is power. For my team and clients, my knowledge can save them time, make them money, and help them to achieve their strategic objectives.

I chose the word *genuine* because I know my team and clients need honesty and sincerity from me if I am to be a true partner in their business. In fact, I *am* genuine. I mean what I say and say what I mean, so that particular word resonates for me.

Those four words come together as the cornerstones of my personal brand. I've thought about them enough to have confidence in their selection, and when I run into my own challenges or wander off the path, they are valuable signposts to get me back on track.

Yes, I know, you have a long list of words that *almost* made it to the top four. But you have to stick with only four. The process of thinking about which words belong and which don't is a critical part of shaping your personal brand.

Record your thoughts. Summarize your results. File it away. Some people like bubble maps, others like loose papers in a folder, or even cocktail napkins. The important thing is the work and thought you put into it. Be honest. Be thorough.

A lot of the information you glean here will go toward developing your brand description in a little bit. But first you must...

## Explore your brand packaging

You've worked the problem from the inside, now work it from the outside. Focus on your outward expression. What does your brand look like? How do you suit up for battle?

You need to perform a self-examination that hits all of the touch points. Break it down into categories: dress, manners, office, car, home, professional tools and accessories. Don't leave a single detail out. Not one.

How do you dress? What kind of hairstyle do you favor? What kind of shoes do you wear? What kind of image do you project? Do you have an accent? Tattoos? Piercings?

Look at everything from clothing to jewelry to cosmetics, nails to eyeglasses to fragrances. Take a look at your professional accessories. What kind of bag do you carry? What mobile devices do you use?

What does your office or workspace look like—is it minimalistic, filled with family photos and things made by your kids, or are the walls and bookshelves filled with certificates, plaques and trophies? Perhaps it is colorful and creative?

What kind of car do you drive? Make and model, as well as type—EV, compact, luxury automobile or pickup truck?

What does your apartment, condo or home look like, and what neighborhood is it in?

What does it all say about you?

Create a collective list of these significant details. Include everything. Once you get everything down, think about what stands out the most.

Go back to your freshman literature class. Think of yourself as a character. What do you see? What are your significant details? How would *you* describe you? Sometimes stepping back can help you be more objective about yourself. Be imaginative in how you approach looking at yourself. What if your life were a movie, and you were the reviewer? How will your biography read? What is your epic poem?

In looking at the character that is you, what "things" most define you? How do they align with your personal brand?

Take a snapshot. This is your best you right now.

Now which of these things do you *want* to stand out the most? And even more important, which of these things *mean* the most to you? How can you refine your brand packaging to better reflect your key attributes?

It's important to note that there are no right or wrong answers. Your brand packaging is just that, *yours*. As such, it should reflect you—your personality, values and personal style. While impeccable suits for men, or high fashion attire and accessories for women, may be appropriate for many—truly distinctive personal brands are unique and memorable and create differentiation from others in their field.

There are infinite illustrative examples within the world of celebrities that immediately conjure up an image—Spike Lee (the activist/movie maker), Scott "Carrot Top" Thompson (the Las Vegas comedian), Dog the Bounty Hunter (the reality TV star), Dwayne "The Rock" Johnson (the athlete/action actor), Billie Eilish (the rebel singer/songwriter), Lizzo (the self-love diva recording artist) or Kim Kardashian (the savvy socialite/

reality TV star). While these may be extreme examples, there's also Tom Hanks (the everyman actor), Brad Pitt (the cool/hipster actor), Serena Williams (the strong, yet elegant athlete), or Reese Witherspoon (the hometown girl actor).

Even within the world of business there are clear examples of personal brand packaging that remain memorable such as Apple co-founder Steve Jobs' signature round eyeglasses, black turtleneck t-shirt and blue jeans, or Warren Buffet's unpretentious, off-the-rack rumpled style and his notable choice to drive a twenty-year-old automobile.

Again, there are no right or wrong answers, so feel free to craft a brand package that is truly yours, and helps to differentiate you among your target audiences and industry. It doesn't have to be overly dramatic either. It can be something as simple as a sharp suit consistently worn with a crisp bow tie, sporting a distinguished handlebar mustache, or always wearing a pair of bright red high heels. These are examples of simple brand package decisions made by three executives—friends and colleagues—who are well-known within my industry.

Ultimately, your brand packaging should simply be *you*, mirror your values, and project your desired key brand attributes.

## Craft your brand description

Next you need to write a description that concisely expresses the core components of your brand—*what* you do and *why* you do it. A big reason many professionals fail to thrive is that they struggle to articulate in a clear, compelling way what solutions and benefits they offer.

Take the work you did for "discover your key attributes," and craft it into a cogent form in your brand description. In essence, you'll be defining your leading attributes, your values, strengths, traits, manners, style, and personal presence.

Start with the basics. Who are you? Age, sex, race, religion, parental status, spouse or partner, nationality, languages/accent, etcetera. What is your background? Where you grew up, education and career history—the highlights. What do you do? What is your occupation? What are your professional associations, civic affiliations, talents, and hobbies?

What is your personal style? Dress, manners, speech, etcetera. What do you do when you're not working?

What are you good at? What are you known for? What are your greatest strengths and traits? What accolades have you received? And don't forget to take a look at what you're not good at too. What are your greatest weaknesses, areas that could use improvement?

Perhaps most importantly, what are your values? *Why* do you do what you do?

Now let's move on to your clients and customers. Remember them? Who are they? What does your perfect client look like? What are the three things your customers most want from you? What are your clients' biggest fears? If you could change one thing about your typical client relationship, what would it be? How do you get new customers? How long does your typical client relationship last? Are they short-term or long-term relationships?

What about your competitors? Just as big consumer brands have to benchmark rival brands, you also need to take stock of what's already in the market. What are *their* strengths? What are their weaknesses? Make a list and include how they position and market themselves.

When you're done, you'll have all the material you need to craft a host of branding tools—your short bio, your long bio, and a host of "stories" you can use.

## Write your mission statement

Thus far we've covered *what you do* and *who you are*, so now we need to cover *why you do it*. It's time to write your personal mission statement, an assembly of words that conveys your long-term goals, and defines how you want to position yourself in the minds of your friends, colleagues, clients or customers, and prospects.

Just as a consumer brand needs a positioning statement, your personal brand needs a mission statement. Here's mine:

> *I seek to do those things that will change the conversation about the hotel, tourism and leisure industry, to upend the status quo, and bring the industry truly breakthrough ideas. More importantly, I wish to be known as a professional whose expertise and advice bring immeasurable value to my team and clients, and directly contribute to their growth and success—personally and professionally.*

What goes into a good mission statement? While there are a lot of opinions on the matter, I'd say that all good mission statements are sincere, focused and action-oriented.

Start once again by asking yourself a series of questions. What are your core beliefs and values? What are you most passionate about? What do you most want to be remembered for?

Sift through your answers and craft your mission statement. Don't worry about the wordsmithing, and don't worry that it's not quite right. Just get it down and move on. You can always go back and adjust it later. Once again, the important thing about the statement is the process you go through to create it, the mental focus on defining yourself in the right way.

Now go back and look at that mental picture of your best self. Does that picture of you match your mission statement? Are your attributes lined up with your values?

How can you change them, so they are more aligned? Once you've achieved that harmony, all you have left to do is to…

## Bring it to life

Now it's time to have some fun. Now it's time to develop the package.

Take a look at the list you developed when you explored your key attributes. How can you change that list to better reinforce your brand? Look at all of the components of your presentation, from your appearance to your professional accessories to your home, and revise the list to better fit your goals.

List the personal habits you wish people to identify with your brand, e.g., always on time, very mannerly, soft spoken, strong posture, great sense of humor, thoughtful, etcetera. You need to intentionally determine your style or presence.

Today's professional doesn't *have* a resume anymore. They *are* their resume. You are a walking marketing brochure for your brand. What does it say? What are its images? What is its call to action? Your brand presentation brings to life the skills you've mastered, the projects you've delivered, and the accolades you've received. Like any good marketing material, it requires thoughtful editing to reflect the ongoing development of you, the work in progress.

This also includes your online presence, which is important too. More on this later.

You need to make sure you understand what picture you want to paint. Once you have a direction and a goal, anything can be changed. A stylist can help you with your appearance and wardrobe. A trainer can help you get in shape. A good salon can help you find the right hairstyle.

Does the uniform fit the mission? Remember to make your brand packaging suitable for your field. Different industries have different qualifiers for doing business, and the right "look" is critical. For instance, as a consultant, I know I cannot walk into an important meeting with a major hotel company—or even a resort owner for that matter—dressed improperly. It's a disqualifier. Although I want to create my own unique image, showing up dressed as a hotel guest rather than a respected consultant, isn't going to work out very well. So be practical in your battle armor.

I remember when I prepared to travel to Ireland as part of my five-year plan—and I wanted to remake myself. I wanted a fresh start and felt the need to make changes in my presentation and image. I had choices to make, as much about my values as about personal branding. I knew I had to be consistent from that day forward, so I thought a long time about my brand as I began the metamorphosis from hotel consultant to college student.

During the year prior to school in Ireland, I changed a number of my brand elements. I bought a big black Kenneth Cole duffle bag, and as I got closer to leaving, I would buy new clothes to match my new brand, and I would pack them in there. Eventually, I put in just about everything I needed, from belts to shoes to toiletries. When I flew to Ireland, I wore clothes I could throw away. When I arrived, I changed into the new duds and threw away the old. I had left the old briefcase and brought a new backpack. I shed my old skin for new. And I did it all completely intentionally.

This is an excellent way to begin to evolve your personal presentation. It's a way to give strength to your intention to change your image. It's a way to make your brand concrete. It's a way to begin to breathe life into the new you.

I recently read that in preparation for his starring role in the movie *John Wick*, Keanu Reeves participated in an exhausting, multi-month boot camp, where he trained to acquire the necessary skills. In the interview, he also talked about wearing black suits for months to help him transform into the now infamous character. Wearing the brand, so to speak, can be very powerful.

I know that the totality of what you have to do to refine yourself can be intimidating. Although it's really a thousand tiny details, you can always begin with one. Create a place where you can physically begin to build the brand—even within a duffle bag—and it will allow for an incremental creation of your ideal state. Maybe it's your desk. Or your car. Or even your motorcycle. Whatever it is, you have to create an incubator for the new emergent you.

## Three things to remember

Now that you've intentionally brought your personal brand to life, there are three keys I'd like to give you: *Commitment, Investment and Consistency*. Together, they can open just about any magic business lock you'll encounter in your professional quest.

**Commit** fully to your personal brand. Take the leap and follow through. Make sure that everything in your life supports and reaffirms your intentions.

**Invest** your time, money and energy in doing things that will further promote you and your personal brand. Get involved in appropriate professional and social organizations by taking on leadership roles. Continue your education and or pursue relevant industry certifications. Become a noted industry speaker or author. Constantly be on the lookout for ways in which you can invest in promoting your brand. Find a way to craft an identity within your environment.

**Be consistent.** Remember that everything has to be part of the vision. Don't alter your personal brand without a great deal of thought and consideration. Being consistent is key, otherwise your team, colleagues, customers and prospects may begin to get mixed messages and lose trust in you and your brand. When something is out of place, trust can quickly disappear.

If you do these things, you are destined for personal brand success. The only question is…

## How far do you want to go?

How aggressive do you want to be? It's time to step out of your comfort zone. Silence your inner critic and give yourself permission to think big—I mean really big, bigger than you've ever dared to think or dream before. Be your most idealistic, inspired, creative, powerful you.

What is your purpose? What is your vision of what you hope to achieve through your work? Remember, your work is an expression of who you are. It starts with small steps, and it builds to massive changes.

Remember, it also takes time to build. You'll probably go through several versions before you find the one that works for you. Along the way, you'll learn a lot about yourself. It's an evolving process. Just don't give up.

## Discovery Exercise

Take the necessary time to finish in outline form the following sentences about yourself. It will be worth the effort.

"I am…" (sex, race, religion, parent, spouse or partner, etcetera)

"My background is…" (where you grew up, school/college, career history—the highlights)

"My personal style is…" (grooming, dress, manners, speech)

"I am honestly good at…" (greatest strengths and traits)

"I am honestly not good at…" (greatest weaknesses and areas that need improvement)

"I am most known for…"

"When I am not working, I like to…"

"When asked about my personal brand, I believe others would say that I am…"

"What I would like them to say is…"

Finish in outline form the following sentences about your clients or customers.

"My clients are typically…"

"My perfect customer is…"

"The three things my clients most want from me are…"

"My customers' biggest fears are…"

"If I could change one thing about my typical client relationship it would be…"

"I most often get new customers via…"

"My typical client relationship lasts for…" (short term or long-term relationships)

List your primary competitors, including their strengths, weaknesses, and most importantly, how they position and market themselves.

Choose the four words that are really "you"—the words you hope will one day be used by your friends, colleagues, clients and prospects to describe you.

## Brand Package Checklist

Take some time to sit and think quietly about:

Appearance
    Hair
    Nails
    Cosmetics
    Fragrance
    Clothes
        Suits/dresses
        Shirts/blouses
        Socks/stockings
        Shoes
        Accessories
            Belts
            Jewelry (watches, rings, chains, earrings, etcetera)
            Eyeglasses/contacts
            Briefcase/handbag

Tattoos
Piercings
Professional accessories
    CV/resume/bio
    Business card and letterhead system (printed and or digital)
    Brochure
    Website
    Social media channels
Car/truck/motorcycle
Office/workspace
Home/condo/apartment

# 4

# *SELECTING A NICHE*

## Finding the sweet spot

*I also hope that I sometimes suggested to the
lion the right place to use his claws.*
—Winston Churchill

*Society is one vast conspiracy for carving one
into the kind of statue it likes, and then placing
it in the most convenient niche it has.*
—Randolph Bourne

*Most people are not really free. They are confined
by the niche in the world that they carve out
for themselves. They limit themselves to fewer
possibilities by the narrowness of their vision.*
—V. S. Naipaul

*Find out who you are. And do it on purpose.*
—Dolly Parton

D eveloping your hero brand is about establishing yourself as a category authority—a known expert in your
field. And it's awfully difficult, if not impossible, to
become a recognized expert in a multitude of fields.

You have to find a niche.

As a recording artist, you wouldn't try to sing country and
opera. If you were an accountant, you wouldn't specialize in personal finance and corporate taxes. There's just too much ground
to cover to be your best in multiple areas.

I learned the importance of finding a niche early on in my
magic career. It's nearly impossible to do close-up magic at a
restaurant, and the next day do a "Vegas-style" stage show. They
both present their own unique, difficult challenges, and they're
two very different markets—and audiences. They both require
different equipment, some of which can get very expensive. I
discovered that those who were richly successful in magic had
found their niche. I also had to choose a niche to thrive. That
way I could invest in the right equipment, and apply my time
and energy in the right places.

Establishing yourself as a category authority in a single
niche will have a powerful effect on the success of your business.
By identifying and focusing on the one thing you most want
to become known for, you simplify and intensify your energies.
You leave no question in the minds of those in your target market about your expertise.

There's little to no risk involved. What do you have to lose?

Having the right niche allows you to choose who you'd like
to bring into your circle. The more specific you are the better.
You can even begin by choosing just one person or company
within your target market to focus on.

Tailoring your market to a specific individual or organization allows you to make the important emotional connection that is so critical in developing a relationship with your potential client. When you've made the effort to speak and write directly to your ideal customer, she'll know and appreciate it. She'll feel as though you truly understand her needs and desires—because you will. It will help to build the trust you're looking for with the clients you want.

If you're not clear who you're specifically targeting, who you want to reach out to and attract, it's hard to market effectively. You'll be chasing after every potential opportunity, and you won't be making a strong connection with anyone. You simply can't be all things to all people. Choosing a niche allows you to stand out in a certain space.

There are many people who have used the right niche to catapult their way to success.

Suze Ormond is one example. She's carved out her market segment in the financial industry. She helps consumers, particularly women, find their way to financial freedom. She's not someone who provides investment advice, and she's not brokering on Wall Street. She's not in the banking industry. She's experienced in talking about specific topics that she knows are of interest to her core consumers. She understands them because she talks with them all the time. In turn, that conversation strengthens her ability to help with advice in the right areas.

In the hotel industry, Chip Conley, founder of Joie de Vivre Hospitality, is a good example of a niche master. He was wildly successful with boutique hotels, almost exclusively in the San Francisco area. He didn't own any branded properties, he didn't want to. He knew exactly who his customers were, and what they wanted. In turn, they came to him because they knew what to expect. He had a process for developing a new and unique hotel experience, because he knew exactly what he needed to achieve. He found a niche in the hotel industry.

I think anyone who has become known as an expert has found their perfect niche, and then made it their own.

What is your niche?

Remember, this isn't about being false at all. Far from it. Before you can establish yourself as a category authority, you have to be one. How do you do that? You truly become a category authority by learning everything you possibly can about the one thing you've decided you want to become known for. There's a change in thinking that must take place. Along the way you must begin to think of yourself as an expert. If you don't believe it, you won't be able to convince anyone else.

A question may begin to nag at you: "Do I have to pursue a niche?" Of course, the answer is: "Yes." You need to in order to compete. It isn't optional. It's a must.

What is *your* niche? In what areas are you currently an expert, or could you become one? In what areas do you need to develop your knowledge of the specialty? What promises can you make and deliver to your target market that will position you as an expert? What promises would you *like* to make and deliver to your target market but don't yet feel comfortable with?

Sure, there are some people who seem to be good at whatever they do. But trying to service multiple niches always splits your interest level. You simply can't be as effective if you focus on too many areas.

Once you understand how important it is to become an expert in a specific niche, how do you go about choosing the right one?

There are three main considerations. I don't think any one is more important than the others, but they all work together in your perfect niche. The first is...

## Do you want it?

It's a matter of passion first. What are you most interested in?

If you don't have passion for the niche, you're certainly not going to want to live and breathe it every day. It has to be something you enjoy so much you don't mind reading all the trade pubs—print or digital—including the dailies, weeklies and monthlies. If you're not into it, the trade pubs will definitely become boring after a while.

What blogs do you read on a regular basis? What podcasts do you listen to? What YouTube channels do you subscribe to? If you have a real devotion to a particular subject, you're more likely to follow through on all the necessary steps to becoming an known expert.

Passion has to be first, but you also need to ask yourself...

## Can I do it?

The niche you're going after really has to align with your talents and abilities. They have to be a match. If you were never into math, accounting is probably not for you, or anything related to true science for that matter. We all have native abilities, and you have to use them to achieve success.

Are you strong in language skills and communication? Are you especially skilled at creating and maintaining relationships? You really have to ask yourself—what do I know today? What do I love to do *because* I'm so good at it? What are my talents?

What skills do I know I can develop further? Am I good at the little things that are required to service this niche?

Without the passion, nothing else matters. And without the skill set, you're going to be spinning your wheels. But there's a third question to consider...

## Is it worth it?

Ask yourself, is this niche worth going after? Is there a place for me there? Is this a specialty that's buried in competition already? If there are currently many experts in this particular area of expertise, is it worth going after? Do you have a unique angle or advantage to help you differentiate from the competition?

You also need to ask, is the market large enough that it's worth becoming a known expert in? Is it a market that could be a lifetime niche for you?

This is where your homework comes in. You need to really understand your
niche.

About my own niche, the hotel, tourism and leisure industry, a lot of people say, "Travel is kind of a small market." Sure, if you're Ogilvy and Mather—an agency for everybody—and Proctor and Gamble can bring hundreds of millions in business, and similar products can add up and you are a billion-dollar company, then perhaps travel is not a good place for you. But they're not a niche business anyway. In my case, I looked at all the investment in the lodging real-estate industry alone. It's one of the largest industries in the world by number of employees and assets. When you consider all of the hotels and resorts around the globe, and then all of the employees, professional service firms, vendors and suppliers that feed the industry, it's a monster—without taking into account tourism and leisure. In fact, the hotel, tourism and leisure industry currently represents ten percent of GDP. So, for anyone to say travel's not big enough, I disagree. Plus, I love to travel to new places with amazing views, and people who carry your bags and bring you drinks with little umbrellas.

But the point is, I thought about it *a lot*. Yes, I wanted it. Yes, I could do it. And yes, it was totally worth it.

No matter what your profession or industry, it pays to find your sweet spot and then become a specialist in it.

# 5

# THE IMPORTANCE OF STORY

## Once upon a time

*A great brand is a story that's never completely told.
A brand is a metaphorical story that's evolving all
the time...Stories create the emotional context people
need to locate themselves in a larger experience.*
—Scott Bedbury

*Forget about PowerPoint and statistics. To involve
people at the deepest level you need stories.*
—Bronwyn Fryer, Harvard Business Review

*Tell a story that is memorable and remarkable and
worth listening to. Seduce your customers, because
that's exactly what they want you to do.*
—Seth Godin

*The universe is made of stories, not atoms.*
—Muriel Rukeyser

We live and breathe story. From the first time humans sat around a fire, we've used stories to entertain, define and communicate about our lives. Today we continue the tradition by reading books, going to the movies, streaming shows, and surfing the internet.

Storytelling is our fundamental language, helping us to make sense of our experiences. Deep inside the life of every person, every product, every brand, every organization is a story that shapes our perceptions. For consumers, it influences how they perceive and interact with products and services. For organizations, it alters how they develop and direct their businesses. Whether conscious or unconscious, people connect the details of their experiences and perceptions through story.

You can't make the journey to your hero brand without the right story. In many ways, your story *is* your hero's journey. The two are inextricably linked.

We're all in the business of persuasion. In order to truly succeed in our professional pursuits, we need to be able to align our cause with others. In today's business world, the most common way to persuade people is with an analytical, intellectual approach. In business, we are trained to deal in facts and not anecdotal evidence. We communicate in PowerPoint presentations, emails and text messages, and we build our case with statistics and quotes. We attempt to cut through the fog of myth, gossip and speculation to get to the hard facts. We think in terms of observations and premises and conclusions, and we favor the impersonal and the objective.

But ultimately this approach falls short.

Even if you do manage to persuade through argument, most people do not act on the basis of their intellect alone. We are creatures of emotion. The analytical approach might excite the mind, but it doesn't connect with the heart. Even though good business arguments are articulated through numbers, they are actually accepted and remembered on the basis of a story, a narrative that links a set of events in a casual sequence.

The right story not only conveys information, it creates emotion and energy in the telling. As legendary screenwriting lecturer Robert McKee says, "Stories fulfill a profound human need to grasp the patterns of living—not merely as an intellectual exercise, but within a very personal, emotional experience."

Stories come naturally to us. They're how we've always attempted to understand and remember the flotsam and jetsam of experience.

Without story, people, products, and companies are just collections of facts, figures and *forgettables*. Without story, it's all just bullet points and endless lists. Without story, it all gets pretty boring.

But if you can tell stories, it all comes to life.

Many people allow their story to be written for them, instead of shaping it themselves. Then the people they interact with respond to this unwitting story as if it were intentional, and the consequences can be difficult to overcome, regardless of the quality of their product or service. Without an artfully articulated story, there is no framework on which people can base their perceptions. They simply can't relate.

Don't fight your natural inclination to frame experiences into a narrative. Embrace and tell the story of your experience to your audience. Make them remember you.

## What is a story?

In its simplest form, a story is a narrative that connects a chain of events. A couple of millennia ago, Aristotle, in his *Poetics*, explained that stories should have a beginning, a middle and an end. They should include characters as well as a plot that incorporates a reversal of fortune and a lesson learned. The storyteller should reveal the story in an engaging fashion, allowing the listener to visualize the action, to feel what the characters feel, so as to be drawn into the events of the narrative.

A good story also contains a fundamental conflict between forces. It features a protagonist and an antagonist, a turning point and a resolution. It chronicles a movement from one state of being to another. A good story has drama, calling on the protagonist to grow and change, to make tough decisions, to overcome challenges, and ultimately to discover a deeper truth.

A good story is not just a linear progression of events. It has to illustrate the struggle between opposing forces. It can't just paint a perfectly positive picture. There can be no story without conflict, and the struggle to overcome challenges. That's what makes a story interesting, engaging and memorable.

As it applies to your business life, it is these negative forces in the lives of your clients that allow you to become a hero to them. So they must be a part of *your* story.

## The more things change...

...the more you need a story.

In the journey to your hero brand, narrative is especially important. It helps to make sense out of what you're doing, to others and to yourself. As you take your leap, when you're in the middle of a career change, telling stories about your professional identity can inspire others' belief in your brand. It helps them to understand who you are, where you've been and where you're going. A narrative thread will help you give meaning to your career history.

It can also help you to believe in yourself. It can assure you that, in moving on to something new, you are not leaving behind everything you've worked so hard to accomplish.

Many people fail to tell their stories correctly in times of transition, and get caught up in the facts and figures. In so doing, we lose a remarkable opportunity. The story of your transition, your journey, has tremendous dramatic appeal.

## Sam's Story

Years ago, I helped a magician friend of mine develop his story. He was an Alaskan Indian who lived in Tennessee, and also happened to be in a wheelchair. He really didn't think he could be a great magician because of his condition. He didn't think anybody would pay attention.

We sat down together and took a look at his life, and worked on developing a story for him. Of course, as a performer he had license to bend the truth, something we don't always have in our professional lives, but the principles of storytelling remain the same.

When we crafted his story, we laid out all the facts, how he'd grown up with Polio, ended up in the wheelchair, and experienced magic as a part of his physical therapy—immediately falling in love with the art. We talked a lot about how difficult it was for him to perform in a wheelchair. He didn't think it would ever work, because he felt that people were looking to see *the guy in the tux*, the impeccably dressed magician who was suave and always in control. He thought people would never buy him as a magician, because if he truly had magical powers, he'd be able to make himself stand and walk.

Mervette Fareed, my mother, with Salah Fareed, my grandfather at the Nile Hilton in Cairo—September 1960.

My grandfather, the former ambassador and brigadier general, Mohammed Salah Eldin Fareed, in North Georgia after he and my grandmother moved to the US to be closer to the family—1990.

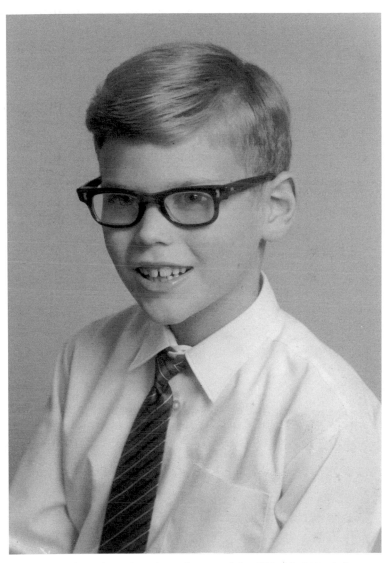

Despite my foray into the US Marines and the "World of Magic," my personal brand package hasn't changed since 3rd grade.

My graduation photo from US Marine Corps Recruit Depot, Parris Island, South Carolina—1981.

Promotional photo for "The Magic of John Fareed"—circa 1980s.

Promotional photo from my final performance in the Parlour of
Prestidigitation at the famed Magic Castle in Hollywood, California—
April 1994.

Speaking at an international hotel Investment conference.

The hotel, tourism and leisure expert in his natural environment in New York, New York—2023.

But I told him that didn't have to be the case. If he were a psychic, or a mind-reader, or something of that ilk, it wouldn't matter. He certainly couldn't be an illusionist, because then he would theoretically have the power to control reality. But psychic powers would work as part of his story. We looked at ways the wheelchair could actually work to his advantage. Maybe he could use his chair as a prop, or involve it in his story in a unique way. Then he would have an act that no one else could imitate.

We started by developing a few tricks that emanated from his chair.

Then we crafted a story about how his ancestors were the spiritual leaders of the tribe, because of their special powers. Each of them, for some reason, had experienced a tragic event in their lives that brought about their powers. He would talk about hearing this from his father, and his grandfather, and how as they each experienced their problems, he thought to himself, "You know, I will probably never be fortunate enough to receive a special gift like they have." As he would continue the story he would detail his experience with Polio, forever being bound in a wheelchair, and lo and behold, the magic of receiving his special powers.

His story was mesmerizing. He made you believe it. He created this profound emotional connection with his audience. At the same time, it made sense of the facts as they were. It turned his misfortune into a gift. We all want to believe that any great misfortune carries with it special gifts. And when Sam would sit and tell you stories, you'd get cold chills, because he crafted them so well. Eventually he was so successful, he was asked to perform at The White House—and today the Middle Tennessee Ring of the International Brotherhood of Magicians (IBM Ring 252) is called the Sam Walkoff Ring in his honor.

## Now it's your turn

Where do you start? Begin by detailing your childhood, your big moments, and the turning points in your life. Create a log of your stories, a written record of the situations that created personal epiphanies for you. Your life experiences provide a rich tapestry of material. You have the right stories; you just need to capture and use them.

For me, I'm half Egyptian. I spent my summers in Egypt. I joined the Marines. I was a professional magician. Then I made a dramatic choice to transition into hotel marketing, eventually becoming the internationally recognized hotel, tourism and leisure consultant I am today. That choice changed everything.

Why are *you* in your industry? What makes you so special as an individual? As a professional? What's your background? What are the things that people are going to remember about you?

You are the protagonist—yes, the hero. Conflict and discontinuity and tension have to be part of the experience. If these elements are missing from your career story, the tale will fall flat. But with all these twists and turns, how do you demonstrate stability and earn your audiences' trust?

Coherence is key to your story. By emphasizing continuity and causality—in other words, by showing that your past is related to the present and that a solid future is in sight. It has to help others to make sense of where you've been and where you're going. If you can make your story of transition consistent and logical, you will have gone far in convincing the listener—and reassuring yourself—that the change makes sense for you and is likely to bring success.

But becoming a good storyteller is hard. It requires imagination and an understanding of what makes a story worth telling. All great stories deal with the conflict between expectations and an unforgiving reality. Without it, there is no drama. As a hero, you must wrestle with mighty forces, and not just waltz through challenges. Yours and your clients. Because if you don't no one will believe you.

You want to be able to communicate your offerings, the benefits you can deliver to a customer. To do that you must engage their emotions, and the key to their hearts is story.

You have to develop your over-arching personal story. But you also need to master a series of smaller stories, the "chapters" of your narrative, that you can use in specific situations.

## The right story can move mountains...and clients

At one point I had a prospect that I simply could not connect with. For the longest time I could not get a commitment from him. Maybe he thought I was too slick—always a danger when you're a consultant, or I wasn't "his kind of people." I knew I needed to break through to him somehow, to help him to understand who I was and where I was coming from.

After one long, difficult meeting I said to him, "Can I just tell you a story before I go?" I saw my opportunity, and I told him the cowboy boots story—more on this later. A lot of other people were around, but I told it specifically to the decision maker that I was having trouble with. And he laughed. He said, "John that's a beautiful story. I love it. Let's go get a cup of coffee." We went to the next room, got a cup of coffee, and I told him one more story.

We had been talking about cars and I said, "I became a Mercedes guy because my grandfather was one. In fact, I fell in love with the adventure of travel because of him too." And then I told him a story about one night when I was about 13 years old, and my grandfather woke me up in the middle of the night. Not my mom, or my grandmother, but my grandfather. He woke me up and told me to get dressed. He said, "Dress nice." We got in his car and I was half asleep, the lights of the city were bothering me, but as we drove it got darker. We drove past the pyramids, out in Giza, out into the desert. Then there were no lights, not even headlights, and I thought, "Is he going to kill me?" I was a little nervous, but he seemed joyous and relaxed. He drove us in his beautiful black 1974 Mercedes Benz 280 with red interior, and soon we were going over dunes, and there we came upon a tent in the middle of the desert. It was made of all these great colorful tapestries. There were cars parked all around it, and there were lights shining through from the inside, and a fire pit with a big calf and lamb on the spit outside. We walked into the tent, and the sand of the desert was covered with Persian carpets, large leather pillows and copper-topped tables. There was a stage at the end with a full Egyptian band, belly dancers, men in white coats with black ties and red fez hats, bringing us food and drinks.

It was a Bedouin party, the nomads of the Arabian Desert. Every so often they put on a grand event and people paid dearly to get into the tent. They live in tents around it, and they set the whole thing up and when they're done, they move on, and maybe head closer to Alexandria, only to come back months or even years later. The whole thing packs up on the backs of camels. It's an amazing thing.

My grandfather and I ate and danced until the sun came up. I got to dance with a young belly dancer. Everyone clapped and smoked their water pipes called hookahs. When it was all over we got back in his Mercedes and we drove back to the house, stopping to get a traditional Egyptian breakfast of *Ful Medemas*—"to go" of course—from a street vendor on the way. We brought it into the house, where both my grandmother and mom were up, wondering where we went. Grandpa said, "Oh we went to get breakfast for all of us." And he looked down at me and winked.

My soon-to-be client loved the story.

I know it was an unusual one to tell but it helped him understand more about who I was, and at least part of the reason I became enthralled with travel, and subsequently, a hotel consultant. That story defined it in a way my resume never could. The next time we met he was a different person. He signed the contract, and a week and a half later I got a nice check.

And that's how important the right story can be. Remember, you can capture people's imaginations on a much deeper level if you toss out your PowerPoint slides and learn to tell good stories.

# CREATING YOUR FIVE-YEAR PLAN

## Time is on your side

*He who fails to plan, plans to fail.*
—Proverb

*Organizing is what you do before you do something,*
*so that when you do it, it is not all mixed up.*
—A. A. Milne

*Good fortune is what happens when*
*opportunity meets with planning.*
—Thomas Edison

*Screw it; just do it.*
—Richard Branson

T his chapter can be summed up in two words: start today. If you wait until tomorrow, you've lost another day. Without the right plan, you can't accomplish what you want in your professional life. If you don't know where you're going, you can't make the journey to your hero brand.

This is your call to action. It's time to put your ideas in motion. Once you've taken the time and effort to establish your plan, there's no turning back.

But where do you begin?

## Start at the end

What do you want to do with your life? Let your imagination take hold, and describe what you want to achieve in the broad, sweeping, magical arc of your lifetime. I know it's a challenge, but taking a look at your lifetime goals gives you a handle on the big-picture perspective that should shape all the other aspects of your decision-making.

Once you have that vision in place, you can break it all down into smaller pieces.

Where do you want to be in five years? Take a picture. Click.

Now break that vision down into component parts. Describe what you see in as much detail as possible. While your professional life is your primary focus, don't limit yourself in your description. Everything is interconnected. Include all the aspects of your life that matter. What do you want to look like? Where do you want to live? What will you be doing? Who will you be doing it with?

Consider all the elements of your life, and where you want to be. Think about it from every angle, and hit all the important categories. Don't limit yourself to just your career aspirations.

Education—what knowledge do you want to acquire, and what information and skills will you need to achieve other goals?

Family—do you want to be a parent; what kind of parent will you be; how do you want to be perceived by members of your extended family?

Financial—how much do you want to earn, and by when?

Physical—how important is your health to you, are there any athletic goals you want to achieve, how long do you want to live and how are you going to make it happen?

Community service—do you want to make the world a better place, and how are you going to help?

Recreation—what do you do for fun, and how can you ensure that you don't neglect your own happiness?

Attitude—is there anything holding you back emotionally, and what can you do about it?

Spiritual—what matters most to you, and how can you build it into your life, and your five-year plan?

That's just for starters. If parts of the picture are fuzzy, that's okay. Focus on the parts you can see, and capture all the details. Then...

## Work your way backwards

What are the milestones you need to achieve along the way? Continue to break it down into specific, smaller goals. Think about everything you've read already, and the importance of positioning yourself as an expert. Highlight all of the specific steps you need to take in your industry to become a known expert.

If you want to be a bestselling author, for instance, you're going to need to know a lot about your subject, as well as the craft of writing. You're going to need to write a book—or several. You're going to need to find a publisher. You're going to need to master the art of publicity. Each of these steps contains a host of other steps as well. By the time you outline those you nearly have an entire process.

## Ready... set... goals!

Make no mistake about it, setting goals is not easy. For a host of reasons, some people find it particularly difficult to sit down and put their vague aspirations into specific terms. But you can't succeed without it. Going through the motions doesn't cut it either, because you have to put your entire self into it. Remember, what sets you apart from everyone else is your willingness to do the tough stuff, like this, when others just won't make the effort.

Goal setting is a powerful tool for thinking about your ideal future, and for motivating yourself to make it a reality. The process helps you, or makes you, choose where you want to go in life. Once you know exactly what you want to achieve, it's a lot easier to concentrate your efforts. Even better, it makes it easier to spot the distractions that could pull you off your path.

Goals help you to focus your acquisition of knowledge, organize your time and allocate your resources so you can make the very most of your brief time on Earth. By setting sharp, clearly defined goals, you can measure your achievements. You can see your forward progress more clearly, whereas before you saw a pointless fog. While that may be a bit melodramatic, setting goals will help you to recognize your own ability to make it all the way to your hero brand.

The good news is that goal setting has a snowball effect. As you maintain the habit of setting and achieving goals, your self-confidence builds.

## Break it all down

As you consider your own five-year plan, chop it up into time frames. For many, creating an aggressive five-year plan can seem like an insurmountable task. But when you break it down year-by-year, month-by-month, you can visualize it more easily.

What do you need to accomplish in each of the five years? Here's where your growth becomes apparent.

For instance, if your goal is to become a best-selling author, it's easy to dismiss it as impossible. But break it down year-by-year, month-by-month, and it's a different matter.

Say your goal in the first year of your journey is to be published twelve times, in at least four different publications—along with a host of other goals. The second year, in addition to being published, your goal is to be recognized with a major award for your writing. In the third, you want to pull your work together and have it self-published as a book. In the fourth, you want to have a book produced by a major publishing company. In the fifth, your goal is to maximize your publicity efforts to achieve that bestseller status. This is a simplified version, but you can see how a seemingly impossible goal can be broken down into steps that are *attainable*.

The important thing is to have a plan.

What do you want to accomplish in your first year? Determine how aggressive you want to be from the beginning. A writer might want to complete twelve articles, or three hundred pages of a book, or three books for that matter, in a year.

Then highlight everything you need to achieve in each month to get you to that point. As I've said before, include as much detail as possible. The process of deciding what details need to go in, as well as what can be left out, is actually an important part of the process. Figuring out what's critical and what's secondary can help you see your path more clearly. If you're in doubt, put it in there. You can always take it out later.

Include all of the things you need to accomplish regularly, but not necessarily daily. For instance, to make it as a writer you need to be submitting on a regular basis, so you might want to say that every Friday you will send off a certain number of articles, or send a certain number of pages to your editor or writing coach.

Don't forget to include everything you need to achieve on a daily basis. These are the things you need to do, and keep doing, every single day. For a writer, that would probably mean reading and writing every day for a specific amount of time.

## Plan to be a recognized expert

Don't forget to position yourself as an expert! Incorporate all the ideas discussed in this book into your goals. Don't just work on your craft, work on presenting your craft. Remember—you have to find your way to your hero brand.

## Put it in writing, and keep it handy

Create a document that reflects all of the steps in your five-year plan.

Make your goals ambitious, but realistic. You don't want to set yourself up for failure from the beginning.

Stay positive. Don't say, "Stop waiting three days to return an email." Instead say, "Return emails within 24 hours."

Be specific. Set precise goals whenever possible, putting in dates, times and numbers so you can measure achievement. That way you'll know exactly when you have achieved the goal, and can take pride in your achievement.

Focus on your performance, not the outcome. Try to set goals where you have the ultimate power to succeed. In business, and in life, there are always things we have no control over—like pandemics or economies. If your goals are based on personal performance, then you have the power to meet them and to build confidence.

Start to prioritize. Try to avoid being overwhelmed by too many goals, and let yourself focus on the most important ones. Then as you revise your plan you can remove the less significant goals.

Keep it close to your heart. Clearly visible on your mobile devices or on your computer desktop. If you still like paper, toss it in your backpack or briefcase. Either way, it needs to be close so you'll be reminded to stay on track, and to ensure that changes can be made easily.

Measure your progress. You could keep a log or journal of what's working and what's not working. Or you could just jot down notes on your paper copy. If there are areas where you consistently fail, figure out why. If you just can't find an answer, ask someone who knows you well for help. If there are areas where you always succeed with ease, maybe you need to set the bar higher, assuming there's an advantage in doing so.

Reward yourself. When you meet your goals, pat yourself on the back. Go to the beach. Take a day off. Savor your success. It will keep you coming back for more.

Check in regularly. Maintain a dialogue with your five-year plan. Keep the conversation going.

## Trial and error

Remember that your five-year plan is a living document. It has to change and grow along with you.

If you're working on your five-year plan, you'll be revising it all the time. You'll drop some goals and add new ones, and that's an important part of the process. Don't feel imprisoned by what you set down initially.

For instance, when I first began my foray into hotel marketing, I wanted to join a long list of organizations and associations. As I progressed, I realized it was far more important for me to maximize my impact within certain niches. If I joined everything, I would spread myself too thin to be effective where it really counted. I simply couldn't join and be active in every association in the industry—there are just too many. So I had to determine which ones had the most influence, which ones were going to make me the most visible, which ones were going to make the best use of my talents. It took some trial and error to figure that out. As a hotel marketing expert that was the Hospitality Sales & Marketing Association International. Later, when I began the migration to hotel, tourism and leisure consulting, it was the prestigious International Society of Hospitality Consultants.

On the other hand, if you're constantly changing the overall intention of your five-year plan, if you keep changing the destination, then perhaps you need to take a closer look at what you really want. If you're uncertain about where you want to end up, then you need to go back and re-examine yourself and your aspirations. If the ultimate goal of your five-year plan is wrong, then you definitely won't get there, or anywhere.

Don't be afraid to remove goals. I've encouraged you to take a very broad, inclusive approach from the beginning. But it's natural, and actually necessary, that certain goals will fall off the list, as you realize what the really significant goals are.

Plan your work, then work your plan.

Start *today*.

# 7

# *FAITH*

## Trust yourself

*Faith is a knowledge within the heart,*
*beyond the reach of proof.*
—Khalil Gibran

*To one who has faith, no explanation is necessary.*
*To one without faith, no explanation is possible.*
—St. Thomas Aquinas

*Don't worry about the mule going blind,*
*son, just load the wagon.*
—Florida Cracker proverb

I n order to make a leap, you have to have faith. When you set out on a journey, you have to believe you will arrive. In order to stay on course, you have to know you can reach your destination.

The world is filled with people who have the ability to accomplish great things. But most of them never will, because they just don't have the belief they can make it. When things get tough, they let their doubts get the best of them, and they quit.

Don't be one of them. Believe in yourself.

Before I got my start, I had no college education. I had never worked in a hotel or resort, other than as Magic Boy. I had never worked in a marketing firm, and had no experience in advertising, public relations or anything that might have made it easy to transition. I certainly had no experience in consulting. I had never given a speech. While I had been a professional performer, I'd never presented anything like a formal keynote. I had never written bona fide trade articles. Sure, I had written articles for the magic trades, but that's a really different game than the professionalism required by the lodging real-estate investment industry.

I simply did not have the core knowledge, and I was well aware of that fact. But I didn't let it stop me.

For me to venture down that path meant taking a dramatic leap of faith. I knew in my heart I could do it. I knew I was going to be able to get from point A to point B.

But where does that faith come from? For me, it comes down to three things: planning, hunger and commitment.

## Planning

It starts with knowing you're doing the right things. Once you have faith in your process, then you can have faith in the result. In my transition, I was able to draw strength from a process that I knew had worked before.

In magic, I learned virtually everything I knew from books. So, when I began my practice it meant going out and getting every book on starting and running a marketing firm that I could find—*both* of them. I read them cover-to-cover. I put one foot in front of the other, maintaining my belief that I could pull it off. I started as a sole practitioner in a tiny, shared office. I turned through pages and pages of magazines and newspapers, looking at hotel and travel ads, and saying to myself, "I can do better, I know I can help." I picked up the phone without knowing quite what to say—cold calling—to ask for meetings with the hotels' directors of marketing or general managers. In short, I didn't really know what I was doing. It would have been easy to cave into my fear, to close the door. I know many people who would have given up right there.

But I had faith in myself. I kept going.

I wasn't the big athlete in high school. I wasn't *Mr. Popular* either—not by any stretch of the imagination. I played tuba in marching and concert band. I was on the chess team—yes, I was a geek, but I went to state. Many of the things I did do in high school however, involved a lot of preparation. I was active in theater too, where we had to plan everything. Select a play, chose our cast, rehearse, build and paint our scenery, and essentially put our show together piece-by-piece. I learned first-hand the value of planning.

A looming performance can bring a lot of fear, so I learned to use preparation to defeat it. In life, we all face similar challenges to perform. When you plan thoroughly, you have the best chance that everything will turn out well.

## Hunger

I believe that people who become entrepreneurs have a certain hunger. They have a burning need to succeed. In your quest to create a strong personal brand you need to tap into that hunger within yourself, nurture it, and let it carry you.

Bill Gates, Steve Jobs and Mark Zuckerberg never finished college. Richard Branson didn't even finish high school. Look at many of the most successful people in the world, and you'll find a surprising percentage of them never finished school. They were too impatient, too hungry to slow down and follow the masses. In fact, according to *Forbes* magazine, the average net worth of billionaires who dropped out of college is approximately double that of billionaires with PhDs.

Often, it's not the kids who are born with everything who go on to achieve great things. It's the ones who come from nothing but have the desire to make it. On occasion you'll see a wealthy family line continue to excel, but more often than not, kids of privilege grow up without the hunger, without the burning need to succeed, without the entrepreneurial survival skills necessary to conquer.

Negative challenges create positive opportunities. Along my road I've faced a lot of negative things. I've dealt with growing up on food stamps and poverty. I grew up in a broken family. I grew up being the weird Egyptian kid in Ellijay, Georgia.

If you have nothing to lose, then you have everything to gain. When you already have nothing, what's the worst thing that can happen? You start over. For me, as Magic Boy, every step that I made was in faith. I said, "I'm going to LA. I've got no friends there. I've got no job there. I don't know what's going to happen. But I'll go and find out. See what happens."

Now, that's almost a mystical thing, and I don't think I can convey it in this book. I don't think I can instill in an individual the strength and fortitude and self-belief that is necessary to make it—develop what I call the chutzpah muscle. But I can tell you that you need to nurture that hunger within yourself and treasure it.

Do you want it? Are you hungry? I know you are because you're reading this book.

## Commitment

I've always believed that when you clearly proclaim an intention to the universe, the results will appear. The world will open up—hence the *Someone other than Goethe* quote in the preface to this book.

Just try it. See what happens.

I know it may sound a little silly. But I've talked to many people about this, smart people in many different walks of life, who really know what they're talking about in their fields, and just about all of them agree.

It doesn't have to involve God, or a mystical force in the universe. Call it conscious recognition if you will. If you don't know what you want to do in life, then nothing around you matters. Because you can't recognize any of it as applicable to your needs and desires. The moment you decide you're going to do something big, when you start to outline your steps, suddenly opportunities appear. It begins a chain of events. Another opportunity appears. And then another.

While on a speaking tour in Ireland some years ago, I was riding around Dublin with Alex Gibson, my great friend and colleague. We drove passed the Dublin Institute of Technology, one of the places where I had spoken. I said, "Man, I enjoyed speaking there so much, I would really love to go back to school. But what would I do? I can't start over and get a four-year degree. What I really need is a post grad."

He said, "You know John, that may be possible. You should apply. Maybe DIT will take you on in a post grad program."

He went on to explain that a number of prestigious colleges will occasionally admit students who can prove they're qualified through life experience, and have succeeded well above others with degrees in their respective fields.

I started to pull together a college application as soon as I got back home to the US. In addition to DIT, I applied to hospitality post grad programs at well-known schools in France and Switzerland. I received letters of acceptance from all of them. At the time, I didn't even know where it would all lead. The world just opened up. But if I had never verbalized it, I would still be sitting here having never gone to school, wishing I'd had the chance to go to college.

I think many people get stuck where they are, because they're afraid to ask for something, overly concerned they may appear foolish or weak. Too fearful to take a chance. Most people lack intentionality in their lives. But you never get anything you don't ask for.

If you truly understand that you have nothing to lose, then every day you have something to gain. Don't be afraid of people doubting you, because if you're not on the right path now, you really *don't* have anything to lose. Opening your mouth and asking questions will never hurt you.

You have to go after what you really want.

## Leaving for LA

As I shared before, one impulsive Saturday morning I decided to take a train to Los Angeles to see if I could make it in the magic business. I didn't know anyone in LA, had limited funds, and no job waiting for me. But I also had no responsibilities and absolutely nothing to lose.

I hopped aboard an Amtrak train, which was scheduled to take four days from Atlanta to LA. Though I tried to plan everything out the best I could, there was a lot I didn't know. For example, I didn't realize I was going to have to purchase my food and beverages on the train. I also didn't know I was going to have to change trains and stay overnight in New Orleans, which was going to cost more money.

I started with about $100, after purchasing the *All Aboard America* rail pass which meant I could travel on Amtrak trains for up to thirty days—anywhere I wanted to go. By the time the train stopped in New Orleans, I was distraught. I realized I didn't have enough money to buy meals the rest of the way, and now I had to find a place to stay. I saw a sign at the train station in New Orleans, advertising guest rooms at the YMCA.

I hailed a cab, headed to the Y, and rented a room for the night. This left me with even less money. At this point, instead of stressing out I decided I was there for the night, so I may as well try to relax, go swimming, and enjoy myself a little. You see, I have always believed that…

## Something will happen

It always does.

While swimming at the Y, I met two guys from New Zealand, enlisted army types on vacation. I shared with them that I was a Marine, and they immediately said, "Hey we're going out tonight. Come with us Marine."

I explained, "No, I can't. I'm on a quest to become a magician, and money is tight." To which they said, "C'mon, we'll buy. We have plenty of money. Come out with us." I went upstairs to my room and changed, and went out with them. Somewhere in our evening of bar hopping, we passed a street performer on Bourbon Street. And then another. And another.

A light went on. I said, "Hey guys, I hate to do this, but I have to go." I thanked them for the beers, went back to my room, unpacked my magic gear—including the obligatory black *tuxedo* t-shirt—and went to work on Bourbon Street. It was a very profitable night!

I stayed at that Y for another three weeks, making several hundred dollars a night on average. On the last day I could leave and still use the balance of my 30-day rail pass, I got back on the train to LA with all the money I felt I needed for a couple of months once I got there.

Having learned how to use magic on the road, I even performed tricks on the train. In the dining, café and bar cars, people would say, "Do another!"

"Alright, I'll do another one," I said. That's when I learned to ask them to buy me a meal, or a beer, in exchange for my performance. I didn't have to spend anything more until I arrived in LA.

I arrived in the City of Angels and checked into the Holiday Inn in Hollywood. I immediately hunkered down and started trying to book auditions. A month and a half went by, but I couldn't land a gig to save my life. I couldn't even get into The Magic Castle. They wouldn't give me the time of day. I was running out of money, and things began to look bleak.

Close to rock bottom, I decided to call my high school drama teacher in Georgia, Geri Worley, who had always been a mentor to me. I shared my whole LA journey story with her. After she stopped laughing, I told her I was going to have to come back home if things didn't look up soon. I'd had a lot of fun, seen and experienced much, but I was ultimately going to have to get a job waiting tables, or head home. I really didn't think I was going to be able to live on what I would make waiting tables anyway. Perhaps I could live in an apartment with five people somewhere, but maybe it was better for me to just go back home and re-group.

She said, "Before you do that, I want you to call my Uncle Bob, he'd be good for a meal." Her Uncle Bob was a schoolteacher in his sixties who lived in the area.

I agreed. I called Uncle Bob, and I told him I was one of Geri's drama kids, and told him my story. He said, "Great, I'd love to meet you, and treat you to dinner." Geri was right. Bob picked me up that evening in an old beat-up AMC station wagon. I was thinking to myself that at least I would get a meal out of it. Then Bob drove through one of the most beautiful neighborhoods in LA, and parked in front of an absolutely spectacular house.

## You never know what you're going to get

Go figure. As we walked up to the house, Bob explained that he didn't want to drive the Mercedes into downtown as it tends to be too hard on it, so he picked me up in his beater. Once in the house, I met his roommate, who was the executive chef at Andre's, a prominent fine dining restaurant. They shared that they had friends coming over for a dinner party, and then added a place for me at the table.

After the dinner plates were cleared and coffee was served, I performed a little magic for them, and told them my story. Shortly thereafter, Bob asked me how much money I had left. I told him I was down to about $67, and would most likely be headed back to Georgia in the next day or two—most likely on a Greyhound bus.

He said, "We have a guest house out by the pool that we'll rent you for $67 a month, including kitchen privileges, if you wish." I was floored. It's at this point I feel I need to tell you that Bob was a stand-up guy, there was nothing inappropriate going on, he just wanted to help one of *Geri's drama kids*.

I stayed the course.

## But what about The Magic Castle?

I stayed at Bob's for a while. I kept trying to get an audition at the Magic Castle, but no luck.

Then something, well, truly *magical* happened.

One afternoon, someone slipped a notice under our front door promoting a neighborhood watch meeting. I handed it to Bob with the mail when he got home, and he said, "Oh yeah, it's at the Larsen's house. They live across the street." Then he looked at me, eyes wide open, smacked his forehead, and said, "I didn't even stop to think about it." He walked me over to the living room window, pointed up towards the Larsen's roof and said, "Look at their wind directional." I looked up, and saw that it was a rabbit in a hat.

I said, "Oh, he's a magic guy."

Then good ol' Uncle Bob said, "No. Not just that. He is THE magic guy. He owns The Magic Castle." It was the home of Bill Larsen, co-founder and owner of The Magic Castle with his brother Milt Larsen.

I almost fainted.

The next evening, I put on my black shirt and pants, red blazer, black shoes, loaded up my pockets, and sauntered over to the neighborhood watch meeting at the Larsen's. It was really just a big chatty social session, so I started performing magic tricks on their coffee table, positioned in front of the oversized white sofa in their living room. In walked Bill Larsen, who sat down in the middle of the sofa and watched me. He said, "Do another one." So, I did, and I went through my "best of" routine.

He looked at me and asked, "Do you know who I am?" And I mustered my most innocent expression and said, "No."

He told me he owned The Magic Castle, and I said, "You're kidding!"

"I think you're pretty good, would you like an audition?" he replied. A week later I auditioned for his brother Milt, and a week after that I got my first real booking. That gig catapulted me into my magic career.

Looking back there are a few lessons here.

One, if I hadn't called my drama coach Geri, who told me about Uncle Bob, who told me about Bill Larsen, who got me the audition at The Magic Castle, it wouldn't have happened. You have to remember to reach out.

Two, it would have been easy to give up, but I didn't. I had faith it would work out somehow. Don't let yourself give up. Ever!

And three, I was ready when the opportunity presented itself. Keep your eyes open for the opportunity, but more importantly, be prepared.

Ask yourself, what is your golden opportunity? Who do you have to meet? What would you do if it suddenly arrived? If you don't know the answers to these questions, you should.

It was the combination of my skill, the help of my friends—and admittedly some very good fortune—that made it happen for me. Your field, your industry, your dream is no different.

# ACT II

---

*Once having traversed the threshold, the hero moves in a dream landscape of curiously fluid, ambiguous forms, where he must survive a succession of trials. This is a favorite phase of the myth-adventure. It has produced a world literature of miraculous tests and ordeals. The hero is covertly aided by the advice, amulets, and secret agents of the supernatural helper whom he met before his entrance into this region. Or it may be that he here discovers for the first time that there is a benign power everywhere supporting him in his superhuman passage.*

—Joseph Campbell

# MARKETING TOOLS

## Wield the power

*We shall neither fail nor falter; we shall not weaken or*
*tire...give us the tools and we will finish the job.*
—Winston Churchill

*The expectations of life depend upon diligence; the mechanic*
*that would perfect his work must first sharpen his tools.*
—Confucius

*Sever the doubt in your heart with the sword of*
*self-knowledge. Observe your discipline. Arise.*
—Bhagavad Gita

*Any tool is a weapon if you hold it right.*
—Ani Difranco

Now that you've planned your journey, you're ready to travel. Now it's time to put your ideas into action.

Positioning yourself as an expert means knowing how to wield your personal brand in the right places and in the right ways. Often that comes down to how you use your marketing tools.

Your marketing tools are all the things you have at your disposal to market yourself—your social media channels, business cards, letterhead, and note cards. You get the idea. But even more important are the more sophisticated practices you'll need to use to establish yourself as a known expert, including speaking, writing and public relations.

As your journey unfolds, you will make use of many of the skills you already possess, but you'll need to acquire new ones along the way. Just as a hero has to have tools and weapons to succeed, you have to master certain abilities to succeed in making the journey to your hero brand.

At the same time, you can't master everything. You'll need to travel light to move quickly. My aim is to save you a lot of time and energy by helping you focus on the most effective ways to use them.

So where do we begin? Remember, no one tool or skill is more important than another; it's all about how they work together to position you as an expert.

## In no particular order

Chapter 9 focuses on relationship building, perhaps the most important and overlooked of all the arrows in your quiver.

Chapter 10 will help you decorate your walls, and put the power of associations and professional designations to work for you.

Chapter 11 is concerned with speaking, and how important it is to find your voice and use it.

Chapter 12 is all about writing, and how to turn your ideas into articles and get them in print and online.

Chapter 13 will show you how to use public relations to your advantage, both in your ongoing efforts and in your strategic thinking.

Chapter 14 will help you to focus your efforts online and use this to build third-party credibility.

Chapter 15 will discuss the importance of awards, and the ways they can gain you bankable clout as an expert.

If you find one area more challenging than another, don't get hung up on it. On the other hand, don't neglect a category either. You're going to need some level of proficiency in every area to achieve the maximum effect; but often you can leverage strength in one area to offset weaknesses in another. The key is to keep going.

## Play to your strengths

If you're a better writer than you are a speaker, begin by contributing a column or opinion piece to a trade journal in your niche. You could even try your local paper or business weekly, if you can position a piece that furthers your goals.

The advent of digital media has created an insatiable appetite for content, as every media outlet today must also have digital channels, all of which require constant feeding. As such, your opportunities to contribute or comment as an expert are growing exponentially.

It's okay to start small. You don't have to make it onto the print or digital pages of the *Wall Street Journal* to get the ball rolling. Industry newsletters, community newspapers, even in-house company publications have columns and inches they need to fill. Once you get your foot in the door—or your name on the page—you've got a track record. Then you can use those clips to get more opportunities in other categories, like speaking or public relations.

If you're a better speaker than writer, try to get an opportunity to speak or participate on a panel at a conference, or *volunteer* to present a workshop. Visibility has a snowball effect, and the most difficult part is getting started. Even a couple of small panel presentations can get you the opportunity to fly solo with a speech. Then it's just a matter of time and effort before you're delivering a major keynote at one of your industry's annual conventions.

As you achieve success with one of the tools—say speaking—always remember that you need to give time and attention to the other categories as well. It's like building a house. Don't focus so much on the masonry that you neglect the electrical; don't embellish the wiring to the detriment of the plumbing. Because...

## It all matters

One of the most important things to remember about your personal brand is that *all* of your actions are important. As you build and promote your professional identity, everything you do—and everything you *don't* do—communicates the nature and personality of your brand. You need to scrutinize everything from the way you handle personal conversations to email messages to how you conduct business in a meeting or social event. It's all part of the broader message you're sending about yourself.

It's a matter of substance, and it's also a matter of style. Often, how you say something is as important as what you say. In meetings, do you keep your contributions smart, concise and relevant? Do your email, texts and other online communications demonstrate that you're current on the latest trends and technologies? What you do is important, but so is how you do it.

Brand packaging matters in a world filled with competing messages. Do your business cards, email signature and letterhead system—printed or electronic—convey your image correctly?

Have you designed or commissioned a best-in-class professional logo, assuming you're in control of that part of your brand?

And don't stop with the tools I've laid out here...

## Create your own tools

Combinations and variations on these themes abound, and you have to use your own creativity to truly enhance your hero brand. A basketball player masters the art of the head-fake, the crossover dribble and the reverse lay-up separately, but it's when he puts it all together that he becomes a LeBron James.

Master the fundamentals, but don't stop there.

Ways in which you can go about raising your profile as an expert are literally limitless, assuming you can find the time. Try to get on the planning committee for an industry conference, or win a seat on an association board, or simply volunteer to be on subcommittee or project team. It's one of the best methods I've found to meet new industry colleagues and friends—and potential clients—while demonstrating my personal brand attributes.

Use your imagination. Try teaching a relevant class at a college or university, or conducting a workshop within a client organization. You'll strengthen your reputation as an expert, and grow your professional status. Perhaps, attendees will think of you for future speaking opportunities.

New audiences, colleagues and friends is the goal.

It's the only way to identify the *right* people, and begin the all-important process of building authentic and valuable relationships. In turn, all this leads to positive word of mouth about you, your brand and your value.

As you gain mastery of each of these expert tools, you will also gain profound gifts: standing, prominence, recognition and power in your niche.

CHAPTER 9

# RELATIONSHIP BUILDING

## Nurture your network

*There is great comfort and inspiration in the feeling of
close human relationships and its bearing on our mutual
fortunes—a powerful force, to overcome the "tough breaks"
which are certain to come to most of us from time to time.*
—Walt Disney

*To be successful, you have to be able to relate
to people; they have to be satisfied with your
personality to be able to do business with you and
to build a relationship with mutual trust.*
—George Ross

*I'm just waiting on a friend.*
—Mick Jagger

Your marketing tools, the components of your personal brand campaign, are really about achieving the right kind of word-of-mouth marketing. In the journey to your hero brand, you should always be striving to achieve third-party credibility. After all, you're not the one who gets to determine whether or not you're an expert. Your professional network of friends, colleagues and clients, is the most important marketing vehicle you'll ever have. What they say about you will eventually determine the value of your brand in the marketplace.

Look at your brand-building tools as a way to nurture your network.

For instance, when it comes to speaking, one of the things I've learned is to avoid standing behind the podium. I've found that when you're moving around the stage, or on the floor walking the aisles—with nothing between you and the audience— they connect with you on a much higher level.

In that respect, I'm more of an emotional speaker. I use body language for effect, projecting enthusiasm—even jumping in the air at times. I make my voice bigger when something exciting is happening in a story. When there's a poignant moment, I try to look people in the eye, and share a bit more emotion, speaking slower in a lower voice. I want the audience to say to themselves, "Wow, I really felt that."

I don't know where that ability comes from, except from experience. But I do know it won't happen if you're standing behind a podium. Ever. It just won't.

As you develop—and hopefully master—your marketing tools, remember that your end goal is to create and form lasting relationships with people.

One of the things I learned early in my career was how to emphasize the personal in my business relationships. When I began to implement it as a philosophy, it changed my life.

As a professional, there are two big things you need to remember in your relationships. The first is…

## The personal touch

When you sit down in front of somebody, don't be the first one to start talking about business. Whenever possible, let them steer the conversation to the important matters at hand. Talk about everything else but business.

Be *interested*, not *interesting*. Be interested in them and their story, rather than trying to impress them with yours.

Pepper them with good-natured questions. What did you do before this? Where'd you grow up or go to school? And ask them fifty thousand things until finally they say, "Okay, here's what we're here to talk about." Great. Mission accomplished.

My former client, and now long-standing friend and mentor, L.W. "Biff" Hawkey, Jr., Senior Vice President of Hostmark Hospitality Group, once counseled me, "Fareed, a person who talks, dominates the conversation. A person who asks questions, controls the conversation." Biff always has the best nuggets, probably why I refer to any time spent with him, as time in "Biff-dom."

Because friendships are at the core of most business relationships, you need to remember to treat matters that way. If you're not already adept at this, give it a try. It will revolutionize the way you do business.

Why?

It brings down the barriers between you. If you meet someone in a business setting, and formal introductions are exchanged, instantly a wall comes up. But the key to forming real relationships is to break that wall down one brick at a time. The best way to do that is to get that person to tell you as much as possible about themselves—personally and professionally.

In the end, it helps them to become more comfortable with *you*.

Of course, there are a host of tips and techniques for personal meetings—leaning in, listening well, not interrupting, making eye contact, mirroring. There are many works available out there that explore this further, so I won't go into too much detail here. But by all means do your reading and exploration on the topic. It will reward you richly.

Don't forget to talk about yourself as well. It's amazing how when you begin to volunteer information about yourself, people feel free to do the same thing. Before you know it, you are friends.

Anyone who knows me, would tell you that I probably share too much about myself personally—maybe you've picked up on that here—but I'm usually well rewarded for it.

I had a high-net worth client with whom I'd grown very close over the years. We traded many personal stories with one another, and found that we shared similar tastes in food, wine, clothes, art and even time pieces. He was a big fan of Cartier, as was I, but the stainless-steel Tank I used to wear paled in comparison to his vintage collectible piece.

One day, I decided to sell my humble collection of time pieces, opting to invest the proceeds into my retirement account, and buy an Apple iWatch. I also traded my Mercedes for a Honda Accord for the same cause. At some point in life, practicality has to win the day, and I was painfully aware I wasn't getting any younger.

A week or so later, I was traveling for meetings with my client aboard his private jet, and he spotted the iWatch and asked, "Where's your Cartier?" I shared with him what I had done with the watch and why, saying jokingly "not all of us are billionaires." He nodded understandably, but grumbled, "a true gentleman should always sport a nice timepiece on his wrist, and that's more or less a toy."

On the night after our meetings concluded, I went up to my hotel room and discovered a festive hospitality presentation on the credenza. It consisted of the typical fruits, cheeses, crackers and macarons, along with a bottle of wine. But I also found a note card and a green gift box. I opened the card, thinking it may have been from the hotel general manager, but it wasn't. It was from my client, and read, "A classic traveler for a classic traveler. Thank you for all you accomplished for us this year, and here's to our continued collaboration." I opened the green box to find a new stainless-steel Rolex GMT Master II, a gentlemen's time piece. I was dumbfounded and grateful, more for the relationship than anything. As you might imagine, I've not taken it off since.

Ultimately it's all about relationships. Sure, you're using an array of different tools to get the message across that you're an expert. Building that foundation as an expert comes down to making meaningful connections with people. That's how you get to be in the right room at the right moment with the right people—because you had the skill set to take advantage of it.

## Be genuine

Here's the rub. You can't be false. You have to be sincere. If you employ a personal approach as a gimmick, it simply won't work.

Most of the time it's easy, but sometimes it can be very challenging. You need to be able to find a way to overcome any misgivings you may have about a particular person—or them about you—and find common ground you can sincerely talk about. You always have to approach interactions with a positive attitude, and project that you're going to do your best to care about this individual, and get to know as much as you can about them.

You cannot act; you have to *be*.

You can't be disingenuous. You can't appear to be establishing the relationship solely for the business end, because it corrupts the whole process. Then the relationship is invalidated, and trust is gone.

In my business dealings, I see that every day.

Just as the journey to your hero brand is not really about appearing to be an expert, but instead actually *becoming* one, establishing business relationships is not just about acting like a friend, it's about *being* one.

When you've met your goal, it's easy to know if there's anything there from a business perspective. You'll have a much more realistic picture of any next-level potential.

When you learn how to truly nurture your network, you are well on your way to your destination. It's important to remember that...

## Networking goes hand in hand with personal branding

What comes to mind when you hear or read the word *networking*? Many find the word cringe worthy as it conjures up *salesy*, or worse, *cheesy* images. But in reality, it's about creating opportunities from existing clients or customers, prospects, colleagues, and even vendors.

## Networking Tips

- Define your goals. What is it that you wish to accomplish during any networking event or activity?
- Define and research your target audience. Make use of attendee rosters, LinkedIn or Google search.
- Make contact through a phone call, email, LinkedIn, or a mutual contact.
- Be sure to have something of value to say or communicate.
- Set up a meeting place and time, even during a conference. Don't leave it to chance—and be on time, *always*.
- Nurture the relationship and build trust:
  - ¤ Be *interested*, not *interesting*. Be interested in them and their story, rather than trying to impress them with yours.
  - ¤ Stay in touch with personal note cards, via US mail. I get that it's an *old-school* approach, but it never ceases to evoke a memorable, positive response.
  - ¤ Share interesting stories electronically around mutual topics or ideas.

# 10

# ASSOCIATIONS &
# PROFESSIONAL DESIGNATIONS

## Decorate your walls

> *A man only learns in two ways, one by reading, and*
> *the other by association with smarter people.*
> —Will Rogers

> *It is easier for a man to be loyal to his club than*
> *to his planet; the bylaws are shorter, and he is*
> *personally acquainted with the other members.*
> —E. B. White

> *Life is partly what we make it, and partly*
> *what it is made by the friends we choose.*
> —Tennessee Williams

T ry this: pick out a wall in your office. Use it as a score-card for every relevant association you join, every professional designation you receive, all the window-dressing of your professional life. Every time you get a *frameable*, put it up with pride. It may seem like an exercise in vanity, but accumulating these treasures is really an important component of your quest to become a recognized expert in your field. Start with your college degree if you like.

Just watch. As the wall fills up, so will the opportunities in your professional life. Why? Because becoming a known expert is all about getting in…

## The right room with the right people

You need to constantly remind yourself of that fact. Joining professional associations is a critical step in becoming a known expert in your industry. In addition to the exposure you get in the local and national chapters of the associations, there are myriad journals and trade publications to appear in, as well as conferences where you can speak.

Think of it as a pyramid, with the associations at the base, the trade journals just above, and the conferences at the top. Your goal is to reach the top of the pyramid, to be a speaker at the annual conferences, but you can't get there without mastering the fundamental laws of associations. Once you do reach the pinnacle, you still need to climb all the steps of the pyramid to keep your status, although it gets a lot easier.

When I was a magician I was a member of the Society of American Magicians, the world's oldest and most prestigious magic organization, and the International Brotherhood of Magicians (IBM), the world's largest organization for professional and amateur magicians. Both had active local chapters around the country, in addition to the national associations. The trade journal for the IBM was *The Linking Ring*, and there were a host of other magazines including *Magic* magazine, the industry bible, *Genii*, published by The Magic Castle, as well as *The*

*Illusionist, The Magic Menu,* and *Marketing Magic,* in addition to many others.

Yes, magicians read a lot.

It was during my career as a magician that I learned the art of maximizing my exposure in the industry through trade associations. I wrote for almost all of those publications, though I really had little prior writing experience. I went to work mastering those trade journals first.

From there, I went to the local chapters of the associations to lecture on my own brand of magic. I sold magic tricks, lecture notes and all kinds of merchandise as I built a name for myself. Eventually I achieved a sort of "B level" celebrity status in the magic world.

Here's what happens. When all of your brethren read about you—or read something you've written—in a beloved trade, all of a sudden they say, "Wow, hey that guy writes for such and such." Or "Hey he just spoke in New York at the XYZ magic conference." Voila, your personal brand value grows.

This doesn't apply just to magic.

## It's a universal truth

Just about every industry has its own trade associations, its own publications and conferences.

When I made my leap to the hotel industry, I literally took everything I knew from my magic career and applied it to my new endeavor.

For starters, I joined the Hospitality Sales and Marketing Association International (HSMAI). I went to all the conferences. Next thing you know I was talking to the industry powers-that-be about volunteering for committees and judging their international hotel marketing award shows. I wrote for their trade pub, *Marketing Review*. I spoke at their chapters and built a name for myself. Eventually, I spoke at their largest conferences, meetings and trade shows from Vegas to Dubai.

One thing leads to another.

Today I'm Global Chair Emeritus of the International Foundation's Board of Trustees for HSMAI and I still act as judge on occasion for HSMAI's Adrian Awards, now the world's most renowned and prestigious marketing competition, specifically for hospitality, tourism and leisure marketing professionals.

Importantly, I also continued to run the steps of the pyramid.

I am also Global Chair Emeritus for the International Society of Hospitality Consultants (ISHC), and I'm an active member of The American Hotel & Lodging Association (AH&LA), the Caribbean Hotel & Tourism Association (CHTA), and the International Luxury Hotel Association (ILHA).

But that's my industry. I know yours offers similar opportunities.

If you want to build your personal brand and position yourself as a recognized expert in your industry, I suggest you join absolutely every relevant association and organization you can within your field.

Once you join you're going to receive copies of their publications—print and digital. You're going to have unfettered access to their online content. You're going to be able to attend their events and conferences.

And then the game is all about discovering how to really...

## Get your brand in the door

Here's a place to start. When you receive the pubs in the mail or your inbox, read the articles and see if there are people like you writing articles, offering opinions or commentary. Are they written by staff only, or do they take submissions from professionals in the industry? Then find out who the editor is. Reach out, introduce yourself and say, "I'm an industry professional. I really find your publication of value and I want to contribute. I've got some ideas for a couple of articles, and I'd love to run them by you." I have yet to find a trade or association pub that says no to that approach. It just doesn't happen. Especially in the digital world we live in today, which is forever in need of new content.

You may find the same names in the pubs over and over again. This is because there are very few people that are dedicated enough, interested enough, smart enough, and focused enough on building their own personal brand to put forth the necessary effort.

If you're intimidated by the writing process, don't let it stop you. It doesn't require transcendent writing skills. I'll cover writing in greater depth in chapter 12, but rest assured there are many ways to achieve your goal even if you're not a confident writer.

If you've never written an article before, trade pubs are a great place to start. They're not looking for an essay, and it doesn't have to be Pulitzer-quality work. It's not *The New York Times*. They're generally seeking about 400-600 words. They want your opinion, direct and to the point. The more conversational, the better.

Why am I talking about writing in the chapter about associations? Because...

## It's all interconnected

When I say writing, speaking and associations, they're all part of the same process. Once you join a group, you're really learning to use the system to your advantage. You're looking for a place in the trade pubs. You're targeting the power players in your associations, figuring out what it takes to get on a committee or the board.

Don't forget to continually focus on your niche. Never allow yourself to become a generalist. What are the articles you want to be known for within your niche? What are the themes you want to explore? For instance, I focus almost exclusively now on lodging real-estate investment issues. That is my primary area of expertise.

Stay focused on yours.

Once you've achieved success within your associations, then you need to go after the right...

## Milestone markers

You should consider going after every relevant certification and professional designation your associations offer.

If you have to be in the industry a certain number of years to prove it, then prove it. If you have to study and take a test, then do it. Whatever your qualifications are currently, push them further, so that you can get these designations. Jump the hurdles. Slay the dragons. Because very few people within an organization will actually do it. And the rewards are enormous.

Think alphabet soup. Earn all the letters you can.

Today, I hold a Master of Science degree in hospitality management (MSc), I'm a Certified Hospitality Marketing Executive (CHME), and I am a member of the prestigious International Society of Hospitality Consultants and enjoy the (ISHC) professional designation. These hold very real value in the industry. There are little more than a couple of hundred ISHC members in the world—membership is by invitation only and candidates are highly vetted. There are less than a few hundred CHME certified industry professionals globally. The elite distinction makes a difference, and you will be recognized for it. When people see those designations they project power and professionalism. If nothing else, people know you're dedicated.

When you've achieved an industry designation, you have a level of status that's simply unmistakable. After all, it's right there in print.

In fact, it's on your wall.

## Exercises

1  Make a list of all the most relevant associations and organizations in your industry. Make your list exhaustive; get everything on the list even though you won't necessarily be able to join everything, especially right away.

2.  Think about other organizations that may touch on your particular industry or niche, or that may allow you contact with other valuable connections. For instance, the Young Presidents' Organization (YPO) or local business groups like the Chamber of Commerce.

3. Prioritize both lists by impact in your given niche, by how much they will further your goal of positioning yourself as an expert.

4. Create a plan to join the top three associations in the first list, and the top two in the second, and add a timetable for becoming a member to your list.

5. Gather information about these organizations and create files for each.

6. Begin to gather names of key figures in these organizations.

7. Research upcoming events and conferences, and think about how you could contribute or volunteer, as someone who wants to add value.

8. When you're ready, go ahead and make casual contact with the key figures you see as the most approachable in these organizations, and explain your passion for the field, and what you would like to offer. Remember to do this with an air of complete humility.

# 11

# SPEAKING

## Raise your voice

*Words mean more than what is set down on paper. It takes the human voice to infuse them with shades of deeper meaning.*
—Maya Angelou

*Everything becomes a little different as soon as it is spoken out loud.*
—Hermann Hesse

*It usually takes me more than three weeks to prepare a good impromptu speech.*
—Mark Twain

In 2004 an obscure state lawmaker gave a seventeen-minute speech in front of the right audience at the right time. Four years later he was elected President of the United States. Whether you agree with Barack Obama's politics or not, you have to admit the spoken word can have tremendous power.

It can be a mighty weapon for you in the journey to your hero brand.

It's true. Once you're a recognized expert, speaking oppor-tunities will abound. And once you are speaking for groups on a regular basis, your standing as an expert will increase exponen-tially. The two are forever linked.

But how do you get started?

I don't want to inundate you with details about the art of public speaking. There are too many other books out there that cover the topic quite well. But I will give you a few tips from my experience that I think will be a great head start as you build your speaking prowess.

The two sides to my process are *practice* and *performance*. It doesn't really matter where you start, in my humble opinion. You won't truly practice until you have the pressure of a perfor-mance before you, and you won't achieve your best performance until you've practiced for a while.

But just for kicks, let's start with the basics.

## Practice makes… well, *you* know

If you're not already accustomed to public speaking on a reg-ular basis, I'd recommend you join a speaking club or group. Actually, I'd insist on it. Before you go out and buy the afore-mentioned books about speaking (which you *will* need to do later), find out which speaking clubs or groups are available in your community.

One of the best is Toastmasters, a nonprofit educational organization that teaches public speaking and leadership skills through a worldwide network of clubs. They'll walk you, or talk you, through the entire process. They'll take you all the way from a baby chick until you're ready to fly, and then they'll push you out of the nest. They have people that have been members for years and love to mentor. There's a true system, a curriculum that can be a real benefit. You're given a workbook to follow. For instance, here's your first assignment, it's five minutes, and it has to be a funny story about your life. It has to have an introduction, middle and an end. You'll be graded on it, and everyone will try to give you positive feedback. It's a priceless experience. There are similar groups worthy of exploring, but my favorite is Toastmasters.

There are alternatives for more advanced speakers as well. I went through Toastmasters many years ago and I'm now a member of the National Speakers Association (NSA). As an organization, NSA is focused on the education, development and promotion of professional speakers.

Regardless, the first thing you need to do is seek out a group that can help you. Once you're there, let everyone know what your goal is. Make sure they understand that your goal may not be to make a living as a speaker. Your primary goal is to become a known expert in your industry. Tell them what you do, and what your industry is. Help them to understand that you're going to be honing speeches targeting that specific group.

Use this as an opportunity to develop your professional material, not a chance to work on your skills generally. Don't waste your time. Don't give a speech about gardening, unless you're a gardener by trade, or gardening is a metaphor for what you do or offers an introduction to a relevant topic in your field.

When you get up you should say something like, "Okay you are all plumbers right now, or plumbing suppliers, or the people who purchase plumbing fixtures and equipment. Because that's the industry and associations I'm involved in. So just imagine that's who you are, and somebody from my association is introducing me." Once they understand the context, it's a lot easier for them to offer valuable feedback.

## Then you're ready to deliver

Ideally, that first five-minute story should be something you can turn into part of your professional presentation. In other words, create that first building block for the big speech. Don't give a generic, random talk. Pick a hot topic within your industry. Tell a funny plumbing story, your hardest sales call, or something that's motivational within your industry that other people would understand. You have to get used to talking to, and about, your industry.

The whole idea is that you're using the group to develop both your skill as a speaker, and the material you'll be using later in your speeches.

## Keep building

At this point, instead of just developing a single speech, work on cultivating a series. Get in the habit of making them topical. Of course you'll want to make three points in your speech if you can, following the classic formula. Start with the introduction, in which you tell them "Today we're going to talk about A, B and C. All right? So now I'm talking about A. So here's A. Now I'm talking about B. And that brings us to C. And I hope you enjoyed my speech today about A, B and C. Are there any questions about A, B and C?"

Aim for about a 45-minute time frame—leaving time for questions and answers—because in most professional settings, like a breakout session or a keynote, they generally want you to fill an hour. You can always pull it back, or expand it, depending on the circumstance.

From there, you should create five or six of these that relate to one another in some way. Eventually you can do half-day sessions and full-day sessions. Once you're there, you can really explore topics in-depth with your audience and build a relationship.

I really prefer now to do half- and full-day sessions, rather than just a quick, hit-or-miss breakout. The bottom line is you want a series of speeches that you can integrate in different ways. The 45-minute framework allows for an introduction, middle and conclusion, as well as fifteen minutes for questions and answers.

The question-and-answer section of your speech is vitally important, because that's where a lot of the true relationship building is done. You can't afford to finish your speech and have no time for questions. If that happens, you've missed a real opportunity to build rapport with your audience. If no questions come from the audience, then have a few ideas in the back of your mind and ask them yourself. Use the Socratic method to further the discussion. It's very important to start a conversation with your audience, to facilitate that interaction.

Then it's time to...

## Hit the books

Now that you've begun the process of developing your skills, you can better separate the wheat from the chaff in the plethora of books out there about public speaking. It's time to visit your favorite bookseller, online or bricks-and-mortar, or even a library for that matter.

As you read these books you'll find some that are really good, and some that are not. The best thing to do is grab a stack, sit down and read through them. Find the ones that really speak to you, that speak your language, and buy them or check them out. You don't need more than a couple.

Most of the better books will talk to you about the structure of the speech. They'll discuss how to build your speech, with an intro, three points and a conclusion. They'll cover how you're going to present yourself, how you're going to dress. They'll examine how to work on your speech patterns.

They may also highlight the best way to moderate or participate on a panel discussion.

It's not rocket science. But finding the right resource books about speaking can provide you with an outline of the process, a framework, so you don't have to reinvent the wheel. It will provide anecdotes that will help you absorb the author's experience as a speaker, and shortcut you to success on stage.

Then you can focus on putting your own particular spin on your material, developing your unique approach, and creating your own original style.

And that brings us back to the power of narrative.

## Remember your stories?

As I develop speeches, one of my favorite things to do after I know my topic is to come up with the stories that I want to tell first. These are basically my analogies, like my cowboy boots story—again, more on this later. All the better if there's a bit of humor or emotion in there. But it has to relate clearly to the topic, or at least transition neatly into it in a meaningful, memorable way.

There are a million stories we all can tell, from our child-hood to becoming an adult to our college years to our pro-fessional lives. I like to spend a lot of time developing these because, in truth, that's what makes a good speech. I've dis-cussed culling and perfecting these stories in a previous chapter, so hopefully you've already begun this process.

Now you need to perfect your signature stories, and think about how to integrate them with your professional topics. In many ways, they're even more important than perfecting your ability to get up and talk about all the technical aspects of what you're trying to convey. While many people can master the technical part of delivering a speech, few take the time to focus on the art of storytelling.

That's why there are few truly great speakers out there.

Now that you're on your way to becoming one, it's time to focus on performance, and reeling in those elusive gigs.

## Start small, think big

Naturally you have to attend the conferences that you're inter-ested in speaking at, both large and small. Get the lay of the land. Follow the same formula discussed earlier regarding asso-ciations. Assess the size of the event, the audience, the sponsors, etcetera. Seek out those in charge, and begin to build some type of relationship.

Show your *passion*. Give them an *offering*. Let them know by saying, "I'd be interested in helping next year (or this year). Is there a planning committee, or subcommittee that I can help with, or be a part of?" Ask them: "If I had a speaking topic I could cover for you, would you be interested? How do I put that in motion? Who should I contact about that?"

The idea is to get on a panel, or get a breakout session or a speaking opportunity. Again, it's generally the same people that present over and over.

You may not make it the first year. But if you keep trying with the right attitude eventually they'll say, "You know what, let's give it a shot." Then you're in.

When you've done it once or twice, people will begin to recognize you. Even if you started at a local chapter, a lot of times other local chapters will seek you out and say, "Hey, so and so saw you speak, and we'd love to have you at our chapter." Of course, it's even better if you make it on stage at the national conference because your exposure is that much more widespread.

Trust me, it's worth the travel. You may not get rich doing it, but if you break even or they cover your expenses, you'll get to add that chapter to your speaking resume.

Generally, in any field, the national representatives of the association are very well aware of what's going on at the chapter levels. Local chapter representatives have to forward their information for newsletters, and online communications. If they start seeing your name a lot in communications from the local chapters, it will greatly enhance your profile on the national level.

Without a doubt, speaking has to be one of the most powerful tools in your arsenal. So let your voice ring out.

# 12

# *WRITING*

## The pen is mightier...

*A word after a word after a word is power.*
—Margaret Atwood

*Writing is thinking on paper.*
—William Zinsser

*Writing is an exploration. You start from*
*nothing and learn as you go.*
—E. L. Doctorow

*I don't like to write, but I love to have written.*
—Michael Kanin

Just as speaking is one of the most powerful tools in your arsenal, so is writing. Article writing is an important way to build your reputation, and a quick steed in your journey to your hero brand.

If writing comes easily to you, then I'm sure you'll jump right in. But if it doesn't, then you might be hesitant to embrace this tool. Don't let yourself be intimidated. Even if writing isn't one of your natural talents, it's a craft that can be easily developed through practice. It's really just another forum to express yourself, like speaking. If you can talk about your niche, you can write about it.

The first step is to...

## Read between the lines

You have to know your way around your publications, both in print and online. You need to read the articles in the major trade publications and journals, and understand the basics—the length of the articles, the tone, and who the authors are.

That will make it a lot easier to know what your target is. And it will make it simpler to determine which publications you'll be most likely to get published in.

Go ahead and select a few favorite articles and analyze them in greater depth. What kinds of topics do they cover? What makes them interesting? What do you agree or disagree with? How would you rewrite them if you could?

At some point you should also create a short list of your favorite authors in your field. Begin to track their efforts and read them on a regular basis; maybe even keep a file on them for reference.

If you're already speaking about your industry, you'll have ideas for articles, but you can never have enough.

If you haven't, it's time to sit down and write five ideas for articles you want to create. Once you have your ideas, it's time to get your thoughts down...

## On the page

It's simple. Don't let the blank page stare at you. Fill it up. Get your thoughts down and go back and edit.

I've written many articles by recording my thoughts, and then transferring it to the page. It helps me to loosen up, but then again I'm a verbal person. I'll get everything out about an idea that I can, and then I'll have something I can work with. Get it all down and then edit for success.

Remember to keep it simple. One thought per sentence. Introduction. Point A. Point B. Point C. Conclusion. If you try and get too many thoughts in one piece, you'll end up with a mess. I'm not saying that you have to follow this formula every time. But if you use it as a starting point, you'll find it a lot easier to write a good article. You'll learn, and know when it makes more sense to break the pattern.

Go with what you know. Try not to stretch your topic too far, or you'll end up bogged down in research. Write about what comes naturally to you. In the end, what you have to say about your current area of expertise is much more valuable to your reader than what you're trying to learn about.

Follow the format. If you want to fill a spot where the article is usually about 500 to 600 words, don't write an article that's 1000 words. You'd be surprised how often would-be writers make this mistake. Sure, the editor may cut where necessary, and there are always exceptions to every rule, but it's best to try and put a square peg in a square hole.

Also, stay away from promoting your company, or your products and services, or anything that leans into being a commercial. That's the surest way to burn an opportunity.

Now that you've crafted a masterpiece or two, you're ready to get your work…

## In print

It's time to contact the editors at your target trade publications and let them know you have some article ideas. Ask if they'd be interested in reviewing one or two.

Don't be bashful. Most of the time the same people write for the pubs over and over again, so they're always interested in new voices. Even if they're not looking right at that moment, they will be. Because there are very few people that are smart and committed enough to do the extra work to get in the pubs.

Again, even if you've never written an article, trade journals are a great place to start. They're not looking for the next William Faulkner, and they generally want short pieces—400-600 words—especially in the digital space. They're simply looking for your opinions, views or observations as an expert.

Once you're in print, or online for that matter, you have to continue to…

## Invest in your craft

Your writing is not a mountaintop you can stand on. Once you've arrived, you can't rest on your laurels. You have to keep climbing and developing your abilities. The extra effort will pay off. If you need help with your writing, get it. Don't be afraid or embarrassed. It's one of the most important skills a professional has, and it touches just about everything you do.

As I've said before about speaking, go to a bookseller or library and pick out a couple of books that can help you with your writing specifically. Read them. Study them. Use them.

There are all kinds of other things you can do to help yourself as well, from writing classes at the local college to executive writing workshops.

If you need to, you can always...

## Seek professional help

You can also hire a ghostwriter if you'd like, and then you never have to write a word. Yippee! For a fee, they'll take your ideas and write a custom piece for you. Your name will still appear on the byline.

But then again, that won't help you develop the divine art of writing, now will it?

That's why I suggest that at some point you collaborate with a writer on larger or more important pieces. White papers are a great example. If you can find a writer you can work with productively, perhaps even someone whose work you've seen in print and admired, you can propose a joint venture. You provide the expertise and they provide the wordsmithing. Then both of your names will appear on the byline. Sure, they'll help you get your articles written and in print. But even better, as you watch them along the way you'll learn about the craft of writing and develop your abilities as well.

So now you've written some articles that have appeared, and your skill as a writer is showing some staying power. What's next?

## Can I quote you?

Here's a useful tip. As you become a writer in your industry, an expert in fact, you need to continue to increase the presence of your personal brand in print. Reaching out to other writers, especially journalists, can really help with that effort.

Let's say your bailiwick is the automotive industry. You're becoming a recognized expert, and you're speaking and writing. You're respected within the trade associations. Essentially, you can offer evidence to support the fact you're becoming a known expert.

Take a look at who else is writing about your niche in print and online, especially the heavy hitters. Who's writing about it in *Wall Street Journal? The New York Times? USA TODAY?* Jot down the names of those writers, and find their email addresses. Get their phone numbers if you can.

Then reach out to them with a quick email, "Hey, I really enjoyed your piece on the latest in EVs, or what we're doing to green the industry, or where we're going in terms of design and engineering"—whatever it may be. Then you can let them know, casually, that this is your area of expertise. Tell them that you speak and write about this niche, that you serve on committees and boards that discuss the various issues. Then let them know that next time they are writing a story about this, or a similar issue, you'd love to help out with any resource material they may need. Or even offer a quote, if they need one.

What a victory you'll have when they take you up on it. Solid gold.

Once again you'll find they're often dying for this information.

Early in my career, Chris Elliot, a prolific writer who covered the travel industry for *The New York Times*, called me many times. As it turns out he also wrote for *USA TODAY, National Geographic Traveler, Forbes,* and a number of other major publications. Today, he writes *The Travel Troubleshooter* which is syndicated by King Features. You can find the feature in newspapers across the country, from the San Francisco Chronicle to the Miami Herald.

I first reached out to Chris in exactly this same way. I've also reached out to other writers at *USA TODAY, The New York Times, The Washington Post,* etcetera. The list goes on. And most of the time, sooner or later, I got the call. "Hey, I'm writing an article, and I need to get a quote from you about…"

"Sure. I'll be happy to help."

They'll never find you otherwise. Most journalists and writers are not going to spend the time or energy to find you out in the infinite stratosphere. They're going to rely on their network of known contacts. Sure, you can invest in listings in the various "expert" books, and more or less buy your way into the media. But in my opinion they just gather dust and no writers I know actually use them.

It's all about who's in their contact list. Try to make it on as many lists as possible. You should keep your own too. Then reach out to them occasionally, maybe every few weeks or so. Don't make it as infrequent as every couple of months—out of sight, out of mind.

Here's another tip. When you see an article that you could have commented on, reach out to them. Don't say, "Hey you didn't call me." Instead, say something like, "This is excellent. I enjoyed the article tremendously, but one thing I would like to have added is XYZ." Add one quick little thing that makes them think, "Darn, that would have been a nice addition to the piece." If nothing else, it gently reminds them you're out there waiting for them if they need you. Don't be obnoxious about it. Just be helpful and consistent.

Eventually they'll be calling you. After all, you're a fellow writer.

## Exercises

1. Sit down and write five ideas for articles you want to pen. Write a brief draft of an outline for each.

2. Look at other articles in trade journals or publications about your field. What do you agree or disagree with? How would you rewrite them? What other angles or approaches would you consider?

3. Make a list of three writers in your field whose work you admire. Write them each an email letting them know you appreciate their work, and tell them about what you hope to accomplish in your work as an expert in your niche. Keep a file on them. Start a conversation.

# 13
CHAPTER

## PUBLIC RELATIONS

### Good news all around

*When you can do the common things of life in an uncommon*
*way, you will command the attention of the world.*
—George Washington Carver

*Some are born great, some achieve greatness,*
*and some hire public relations officers.*
—Daniel J. Boorstin

*I read the news today, oh boy.*
—The Beatles

In many ways, your entire quest to position yourself as a known expert is about public relations. You wield your prowess in relationship building, speaking, writing and being quoted, in an effort to be recognized by third-party sources as a category authority.

Most professionals believe they understand public relations well. Just about everyone knows how to write a press release. We all appreciate the importance of forging relationships with

117

those who report on our sphere of business. We understand how beneficial it is to get our names in print and online in the right places.

Few, however, really understand how to maximize the power of public relations and reap its benefits for their personal brands. Hardly any know how to find the pressure points, the hot buttons, and apply them in the right way at the right time to make a memorable—and measurable—impact.

Here's the truth. Unless you are a big publicly traded company, or someone who's doing something truly innovative on an ongoing basis, publications are only going to write about you once. They may revisit you every two or three years, max, because the editors are going to say, "We've already covered him, let's move on." Even big players in their industries can suffer from this syndrome.

What most professionals are looking for is maximum coverage in their industry press. This includes the trade journals, association publications, and all the online vehicles that cover their milieu on a regular basis, and perhaps the local press and business magazines. They want coverage in any medium that regularly speaks to their clients and prospects.

How do you make public relations work for you on that level?

As previously discussed, one great way to start is to write for them. You build your credibility, get your photo in, your company name, and that blurb about what you do. Been there.

The second way is to be a speaker at their conferences. Once again your personal brand as an expert makes an appearance, and you get a small opportunity to talk about yourself and your company, and hopefully some successes. Done that.

Finally, the third way is to do something they'll write about. That's the heart and soul of public relations. And there are all kinds of things that will get you press.

The way I see it, there are two sides to PR. The first side of the coin is...

## Ongoing... and going

And going. That's the side of PR that you need to make happen all the time. Your "no-brainer" efforts you need to create and maintain on a regular basis. Your press kit. The materials you create and post to your company web site.

Then there are the press releases about all the "news"— new clients, new projects, new offices, and new hires. If you're a plumber and you just won the contract for a big, new commercial project, you write about it. If you're in lodging real-estate investment and you just won a development consulting assignment for a big new hotel or resort, you write about it. If you're a big enough company and you just brought a new c-suite executive on board, you get their headshot and bio and you write about it.

You send them out to the trade and local business publications, to the editors or the vendor news department, or whatever it may be, and you get a little paragraph or two.

To keep this rolling, to be a successful PR aficionado, you or your organization need to have a system in place. Maintain a list of every media contact that you're going to be submitting to continually. This includes the business and trade press, and their online incarnations, as well as anyone else you believe needs to stay in the know. Most of the time, they're generated electronically and sent out the same day. If you do that every other week, or even once a month, you could end up with dozens of meaningful media hits a year.

## Let no story go untold

If you or your company is doing something that's unique and interesting, by all means talk about it. Just remember to always strive for a fresh angle, if you want it to make it in print or online in third-party mediums.

Examples include: we experienced 486% year over year sales growth, opened a European office, got a new partner, won an large assignment from a Fortune 500 company, or just celebrated our 30th year in business. These are all ideas that can be crafted into stories, and may win you coverage. You may even create enough interest to win a feature article.

Again, this is a process that you can research and adapt to your needs. This is ongoing PR.

On the other side of the coin is, in my opinion, the stuff that *really* matters. That's the side of PR that's all about...

## Strategic thinking

What are your key marketing messages? What is going to truly position you as an expert? What are you doing right now, as a company or as a personal brand, that you can leverage to reinforce those marketing messages and your role as a category authority? How can you use it to underscore your emergence as a hero brand?

Again, there are a slew of books about ways to get your brand in the press. But how can you achieve maximum impact? It starts by not being satisfied with just getting your name in print, but focusing on finding ways to position yourself as an expert—strategically.

The idea is to save your best efforts and opportunities for the most *strategically beneficial* opportunities. You can spend a lot of time and energy detailing every little thing you and your company do, every bit of news, but the real key to achieving maximum impact is to get your name positioned in the *right* way.

For example, keep your eyes and ears open for "what's hot." Find a way to tap into your industry's emerging trends, challenges, and concerns, and leverage them into media opportunities. You can do it. The truth is that just about anyone, in just about any industry, can identify and leverage these kinds of media opportunities to position themselves as an expert.

In the journey to your hero brand, you don't want to get waylaid doing a host of things that drain your time and energy, even if they're important tasks in their own right. Public relations, like social media, can be a trap. That's why I highly recommend you save yourself for the most strategic endeavors. Part of that approach means handing off a lot of your public relations activities, and harnessing the...

## Power of a media relations expert

If you really want to establish your place as a known expert in your field, if you really want to make the journey to your hero brand, you may want to hire a media relations expert.

Go ahead and put one on retainer, even if it's only for a few months. Hire them. Tell them what your goal is. Let them craft a plan for you they can initiate and maintain.

You can save yourself months of work.

Media relations experts are generally very accessible and easy to work with. There are associations, such as the Public Relations Society of America, that can recommend local free-lancers or small firms to assist with your public relations efforts.

PR is both a relationship game and a creative process. A good PR professional will have connections that will take *you* a very long time to forge. They'll be better able to find ways to place you in the media, and they can establish your ongoing activities for you, so it becomes mechanical. Much of the important work for a major PR campaign can be completed within a few months by an effective and seasoned media relations expert. Then you can re-hire them when the time comes for your next campaign.

The mechanics of PR can be a tricky business, and the devil is truly in…

## All the details

That's why, as an expert in your field, you need to have all the publicity tools ready when you need them. You'll need:

- A full bio (not a CV but a genuine bio, crafted by you, a copywriter, or a PR professional)
- A good headshot, in both low-resolution (for digital purposes) and high-resolution (for print)
- A well-crafted fact sheet on you and your company
- A list of awards
- A list of certifications and what they mean
- A list of pubs for which you've written
- A list of media venues where you've been quoted or featured
- A list of conferences where you've spoken

You'll need to keep these active and alive, and attend to them on a regular basis. You're going to need them—don't just rely on your LinkedIn profile. At some point someone is going to ask you where you've spoken or written or been quoted as an expert, and then you'll have it ready. You'll need it for your press kit. You'll need it when you're speaking, and when you're submitting an article. You'll need it when you have PR opportunities, and you'll need it when someone wants to quote you. And they *will* want to quote you.

I don't show these to everybody, but I keep them handy. I revise them on a regular basis. If anyone asks what I'm up to, I can pull out what I need at a moment's notice.

Because you always have to be ready to make some news.

# 14

# ONLINE

## How the web was won

> One of the internet's strengths is its ability to help consumers
> find the right needle in a digital haystack of data.
> —Jared Sandberg

> The internet is becoming the town square
> for the global village of tomorrow.
> —Bill Gates

> The internet is the first thing that humanity has
> built that humanity doesn't understand, the largest
> experiment in anarchy that we have ever had.
> —Eric Schmidt

> Give a person a fish and you feed them for a day; teach that
> person to use the internet and they won't bother you for weeks.
> —Unknown

To be honest, I really didn't want to write this chapter. Because by the time this book is published, more than likely all the tools I'd love to suggest right now will have changed in one way or another.

That's how fast the cyber-currents move. New tools emerge and gain popularity, and just as you figure out how to make them work for you, they're replaced by newer, even better tools.

It's easy to get caught up in the churn. You can waste a lot of valuable time paddling in the wrong direction.

That doesn't mean you shouldn't strive to master the power of the internet. You should, but that topic deserves an entire book of its own. A digital one. Posted on the Net. Updated every day. Maybe several times a day.

But I had to include this chapter because there are a few key points you need to consider on the journey to your hero brand.

Let's start with the basics. You need to...

## Put your best page forward

Yes, your company must absolutely have a website—what company doesn't? And it has to sing with the same professional panache and style as all of the rest of your company's marketing tools and materials. It should contain the substance of your personal brand wherever possible too, the essence of your mission and your value proposition, and ideally be a showcase for your best work or experience—even if only in your profile within the *team* or *about us* pages.

All of that's a given.

Yes, your site should include all of the key words and phrases that are critical to your company, and you as an expert in your niche. Yes, you should offer your linguistic sacrifices to the gods of SEO.

All I'm saying is that you shouldn't get too carried away.

You see, one of the best things about the cyber revolution is that...

## Anyone can do it

First, the good news. The internet has made it a lot easier for all the "average Joes" to position themselves as experts. With a little knowledge and time, just about anyone can create a website, or produce a podcast. If they're skilled enough, they can build a following via one or more of the seemingly infinite choices of free social media channels available today. The barriers to entry have come crashing down.

The bad news? Just about *anyone* can do it.

So, when it comes to your web presence, you need to understand you're essentially on the same level playing field as all of the wannabees, dilettantes and competitors out there. That's the truth.

How do you show you are a legitimate expert in your niche? Let me ask you, when you visit websites, how do you separate the players from the pretenders—the best from the rest? Most of the time, whether consciously or unconsciously, we all rely on that old familiar standby—third party credibility.

Anyone can produce a podcast. There's no qualifying standard. You can get started today and build web traffic. But not everyone can get on CNN or MSNBC, or in my industry hotelnewsnow.com.

It's one thing to discover a site out of the blue in a Google search. It's entirely different to arrive there via a link in *The Wall Street Journal* or *Lodging* magazine. That's an extreme example, but we have a real tendency to value sites more that are linked to other credible sites, or that we've read about or discovered in mass media.

That's why it's important to remember that the credibility of your web presence is still based on the matrix of other personal branding tools in your arsenal—your speaking, writing and public relations.

It's great to post your articles and content on your site, and sometimes they'll even be picked up and posted to other sites. But I still think it's better to...

## Go where the action is

For you to be seen as a known expert, you have to constantly strive for the greatest recognition from the marketplace you can achieve.

Remember, *you* don't get to decide that you're an expert. Others have to do that for you. And because your resources are finite, you have to maximize the impact of everything you do. The marketplace alone determines whether you're an expert. You can *say* you're an expert, but no one's going to consider you an expert until a third party says "this is the guy," or "she's the end-all, be-all on the topic." Then, when you appear in major media, or at conferences as a speaker, you are endorsed and validated as someone who's knowledgeable.

What has more influence: an article, white paper or report you posted on your own site, or one that's been posted on msnbc. com? Or fastcompany.com? Or for me, hotelbusiness.com?

You still want to be on television. You still want to be writing and getting your articles published. You still want to be speaking at major conferences. You still want to be relevant in the marketplace. But the only people who are going to make you relevant, are those well-known third parties that consumers and prospects value.

Horwath HTL is a structured network of member firms— *250 senior consultants with strong personal brands*—connected through membership in our parent company, Crowe Global, the 8th largest global accounting network in the world by revenue.

Our website features robust news and publications sections. We collectively spend a lot of time creating content for them, some of which is occasionally picked up by the media. While this is great, we always strive to have our publications and content spotlighted by major industry media outlets from the beginning. Our site will never achieve the number of visitors they do. That's why we go after third parties first. It takes the same amount of energy. Afterward, we post them on our site, with permission of course, and say, "as it appeared on hotelnewsnow.com." That gives us the third-party credibility as industry experts that we're all seeking.

Don't make the mistake of just putting everything you create on your own site. You still have to get your name out there. You still need to be actively pursuing third party credibility—then promoting it on your own website and social media channels.

Yes, at Horwath HTL we use social media too, but only for promotional support. We post and tweet about our speakers and attendees at industry conferences, member articles and interviews in industry media, as well as new reports and publications we've authored. On occasion, we'll post an opinion or POV—point of view—piece. But essentially, we use social media as a promotional tool.

You must carefully select the right platforms and messaging for you and your organization. Identify the social media platforms where your target audiences are most active. The most popular options for business, as of this writing, include LinkedIn for professional networking, Instagram for visual content, and Threads for sharing insights and engaging in conversations.

Regularly post content that aligns with your company and personal brand, and provides value to your audience. This could include sharing insights, industry news, tips, or engaging in conversations. Use a mix of text, images, videos, and other media formats to make your content more engaging.

Speaking of engaging, you should make sure you interact with others. Actively participate in discussions, comment on relevant posts, and *connect* with your audience. This helps build relationships, expands your network, and demonstrates your expertise.

Network strategically. Reach out to industry professionals, thought leaders, and influencers in your field. Engage with their content, share their posts, and contribute to relevant conversations. This can enhance your visibility and reputation within your industry.

Monitor your online presence. Regularly check your social media profiles and respond promptly to comments, messages, and mentions. Address any concerns or negative feedback professionally and transparently.

Leverage multimedia content. Experiment with different types of media to make your brand stand out. Create videos, infographics, or podcasts that showcase your expertise and offer unique insights.

Finally, a word of caution. Please remember that everything you post will be out there…

## Always and forever

Yes, whatever you post is out there for eternity. It's not going anywhere. It will live somewhere on the web forever. That's why, in terms of your own website, podcasts and social media, sometimes less is more.

Make sure that *everything* you create and post lines up with your hero brand.

# 15

## *AWARDS*

### And the winner is…

*Without ambition one starts nothing. Without work one
finishes nothing. The prize will not be sent to you. You have
to win it. The man who knows how will always have a job.
The man who also knows why will always be his boss.*
—Ralph Waldo Emerson

*Hollywood has its Oscars. Television has its Emmys.
Broadway has its Tonys. And advertising has its Clios.
And its Andys, Addys, Effies and Obies. And 117 other
assorted awards. And those are just the big ones.*
—Joanne Lipman

*Most awards, you know, they don't give you unless you go
and get them–did you know that? Terribly discouraging.*
—Barbra Streisand

H ere's the deal. Every industry has its awards. And
winning them is a great way to position yourself
as an expert. But you can't get them unless you go
after them.

130

You would be astonished how many successful professionals do not even consider award competitions in their industries. In fact, many people *disdain* the idea of even entering them.

Here's the question: do these same people have respect for the people who do win awards in their industries? Absolutely. You bet.

Sure there are exceptions to the rule. There are always controversies over whether certain people deserve recognition. But for the most part we have respect for those who win awards, because we believe they have indeed earned them.

So in pursuit of your standing as an expert you have to embrace the idea that you must go after awards and recognition in your industry. You are a hero brand. You have to make sure you are recognized for it.

But you can't get the prize if you don't throw your hat (and heart) into the ring. You have to be...

## In it to win it

It's true. Most awards you have to enter to win. Even the ones that don't have a formal entry process, that rely on nominations from association members or leaders in the market, still require some effort on your part to get the ball rolling.

No one is going to nominate you for an award unless you're on their radar in the first place. A well-placed gentle suggestion is often all that's needed to turn someone in your direction. The rewards are well worth the effort.

In just about every industry there are prominent awards that you can win. But first you need to figure out...

## What's out there?

Many of the big awards in your field won't be easy to attain at the beginning, but there are almost always some categories where you can compete right from the get-go.

For instance, there's the *Volunteer of the Year* award, which is often highly respected within a group because it represents substantial time and energy put forth by the recipient for the good of all members. These are also traits that dovetail nicely with the emergence of your hero brand, and a lot of things you need to do to win that award you should be doing anyway. That echoes our core principles of *passion* and *offering*, the keys to success in your trade associations.

Now, every association is different, and some won't really consider you until you've been in the association for a long time. But that's okay, there are others. If you think about what it takes to win that award from the beginning, you'll be that much further along in your pursuit of achieving it down the road. When you do win it, the value will be tremendous, and you'll undoubtedly garner a lot of press.

There are many others. Take the time to explore and do an exhaustive search. Brainstorm all the possibilities in your trade associations and your community. Think about it from all angles.

In my industry and others there are numerous *Deal of the Year* and *Development of the Year* awards. Have you done anything recently that might qualify? Is there anything on your horizon that might be considered an entry? By asking yourself these questions, you've already begun to change the way you think about your business and the pursuit of these kinds of opportunities.

There are *advertising and marketing* awards. One of the great things here is that there is usually a range of categories to choose from. If you don't have anything to enter right now, ask yourself how you can tweak your activities for next year to make sure you can enter something. This is also a great way to start small as you progress to bigger awards.

There's the *Salesperson of the Year* award. A friend of mine won *National Salesperson of the Year*, number one in his organization in the whole country, and he appeared in all the major trade pubs in his industry.

Of course, we all want that *Lifetime Achievement* award, the pinnacle of expertdom. When you win that award no one can dispute that you have arrived. Sure, it may take a long time, but you'll never get there if you don't start down the path now by building you brand and protecting your legacy.

And there are other ways to get recognition, too. You can also begin to...

## Rise up the ranks

Rankings are everywhere. The media loves them.

For instance, my firm was ranked highly in a trade publication comparing consulting firms. The other firms on that list were pretty impressive, and I'm proud to have our name appear next to theirs. In addition, there were key competitors in my niche that were not on the list.

There are too many *types* of rankings to even mention here. Things like *Top 40 Under 40* or *50 over 50*. Trade pubs frequently compile and write about them, and local business magazines and even other trade publications use them.

There's *Most Influential in Business*. And the subsets that extend from that like *Most Influential Businesswomen*. The list goes on and on. For ideas, take a look at your trade journals and local business press over the last couple of years. Every industry is different.

## You deserve it

Remember all the work you have put into your professional career? Hold fast to all the things you have done, not only to position yourself as an expert, but to *become* one.

No one will recognize you as a winner unless *you* believe you *are* one, and act accordingly. That applies to just about everything in life, and especially to awards and rankings within your industry.

Now go win one for your hero brand.

# ACT III

*The adventure is always and everywhere a passage beyond the veil of the known into the unknown; the powers that watch at the boundary are dangerous; to deal with them is risky; yet for anyone with competence and courage the danger fades.*
—Joseph Campbell

# 16

# CHALLENGES

## Enter the villains

> *There is no such thing as a problem without a gift for you*
> *in its hands. You seek problems because you need their gifts.*
> —Richard Bach

> *Great spirits have always encountered violent*
> *opposition from mediocre minds.*
> —Albert Einstein

> *An excellent man, like precious metal, is in every way*
> *invariable. A villain, like the beams of a balance,*
> *is always varying, upwards and downwards.*
> —John Locke

I am a positive person. For me, the glass is *always* half-full, or even completely full, for that matter. It's not something I've worked on or trained myself to become, it's just who I am.

I suspect that you're the same. That's how most of us became leaders in business—we could visualize and achieve positive outcomes where others might have quit.

But even for positive people, not everything is perfect all the time.

Every hero has a series of challenges to overcome. There will always be roadblocks and potholes, wrong turns and highway robbers.

The further along you get in the journey to your hero brand, the more likely you are to confront these negative forces. The closer you get to your destination, the more intense they will become.

Most of these challenges will come from the outside world. There will be the inevitable attacks from competitors, detractors and their ilk. People whom, for one reason or another, resent your rise to become a recognized expert in your field.

There will be challenges that will come from within as well. One of the biggest internal obstacles is…

## Self-doubt

It's a double-edged sword. Anxiety and uncertainty can unravel some people, making them lose faith in the good plans they've created, often for no reason. *Unreasonable* self-doubt can erode your confidence, a quality that no hero can do without.

On the other hand, a healthy measure of self-doubt, tempered with reason, can be a strength. It can be the voice that says, "Check the ropes on your sails one more time." That final check can be what saves you when you're on the open sea.

If you don't have moments of self-doubt every day, then you probably aren't really challenging yourself.

I have moments of self-doubt. Sometimes I get up and wonder if I'm really going to be able to pull everything together today. There are times when I know I have to get up in front of an audience and I feel a lot of uncertainty, and then I blow everyone away, including myself. There are other times when I feel *no* self-doubt, and my speech is just okay. Sometimes being a little nervous is an advantage, especially in any kind of performance.

Self-doubt is good. It means you're thinking, looking at all the problems that could occur. Self-doubt means you're looking at your shortcomings. It means you're not fooling yourself.

You don't want the surgeon who comes into your room in the hospital and says, "I have no self-doubts about your surgery." Personally, I want the one who is thinking "I need to make sure I do this correctly, that I stay focused, that I absolutely know what I'm doing, and will do my best to ensure this will be the best procedure I've ever done." I don't want the guy who is 110 percent sure he knows everything, who thinks that he's in complete control. The minute you say you're in total control, you're probably *not*. It says to me you haven't thought everything through.

I've always liked people, especially in important positions, who have a bit of self-doubt and aren't afraid to show it. A lot of the time self-doubt is self-awareness. Sure, confidence is important. But I like people that are realistic.

The trick is to listen to your doubts, but not let them overcome you. Think them through and check the ropes. Then get on with your journey.

Planning is important. If you've laid your plans carefully, then you'll understand where you may have problems, and you'll anticipate some of the solutions. If you've invested the time in your planning, you'll have a lot more confidence when you encounter those inevitable obstacles.

Everyone's faith is challenged at some point. But if you've done your homework in your planning, you can go back to those conclusions and take a reasonable look at where you are. Most of the time, it will keep you on the right path.

A reasonable look at your self-doubts will also allow you to adjust your plan when you need to. You're much more likely to be able to separate the difficulties of circumstance from a real flaw in your plan.

And remember that...

## Every mistake is a blessing

When I began my five-year plan to become an expert, I felt like I'd made enough mistakes already to fill several lifetimes. Because of that, I felt like I could face just about anything the world could throw at me. A lot of businesspeople will tell you life is always better the second time around, because you know so much more.

With my five-year plan, I was so committed that I never had second thoughts about the plan itself. I may have had concerns about the component parts—"I hope I graduate." "I hope I can make it a year at this firm." But those concerns were my own way of telling myself, "Make sure you graduate," "Make certain you make it a year." That's a good thing.

There were steps along the way when I had self-doubt, not about whether it was the right thing to do, but about whether or not I could pull it off. "At my age, can I live in an employee dorm for a year or longer?" As long as your goal is truly what you want, as long as your aim is true from the beginning, the answer is *always*, "Yes, you can."

Remember that. You wouldn't have this dream if you couldn't do it. You wouldn't have started down this path if you didn't really want it. In times of trouble, you just need to remind yourself of this.

Use those self-doubts to your advantage. If you have areas you're concerned about, address them. Don't just worry. Make the necessary changes if you need to. Look around for the new opportunity that may be hidden there.

But even if you conquer the forces of doubt within, you also have to face…

## Hostile forces

In my professional career, nothing surprises me more than the lengths to which other people will go to pull you down. It's been quite a lesson for me. I'm sure that in your pursuit of becoming a known expert in your category, or whatever it is you're trying to accomplish, you'll experience the same.

Most of the time it will be other individuals within your industry—competitors—that will try to pull you down. They'll try to disparage you. They'll concoct stories about you. They'll try to paint you in a bad light. They'll take advantage of every opportunity to pull you back down to their level, to keep you from rising.

I'm sure you'll run into people like this, if you haven't already. As I said before, the higher up you go as an expert in your field, the more intensely some will try to bring you down.

What do you do?

For one thing, it's important not to allow this kind of activity to alter your plans. Don't allow these cheeky, negative professionals to change how you go about pursing your dreams. Eventually their assaults will backfire on them.

You just have to drag them...

## Into the light

Whenever possible, don't allow them to operate behind the scenes. Face them head on. If someone tells a false story about you, confront them. If someone is telling you one thing, but telling a business associate another, get them both on the phone at the same time. Or meet with them. Pull them into the light. I have found that deceitful people often wilt under this kind of exposure.

Most of the time these shenanigans are exposed anyway. It's just a matter of time; you simply have to wait it out. Eventually, your consistently positive actions will be evident to everyone. I can't guarantee it. But in my experience, it almost always works out that way.

Remember earlier in the book when we talked about how important it was to build your relationships? Those relationships will come to your rescue in tough times like these. When your name is under attack, those who know you and your true character will be there to defend it. The best defense against a smear campaign is the sterling reputation you've already earned.

Weather the attacks. Stick to your guns. Stay on the path to your hero brand. Once the light comes on, the villains will scatter.

# 17

# DEVELOPING YOUR FAN CLUB

## A little help from your fans

*Remember, no man is a failure who has friends.*
—George Bailey, *It's a Wonderful Life.*
*There is great comfort and inspiration in the feeling of
close human relationships and its bearing on our mutual
fortunes—a powerful force, to overcome the "tough breaks"
which are certain to come to most of us from time to time.*
—Walt Disney

*Keep away from those who try to belittle your ambitions.
Small people always do that, but the really great
make you believe that you too can become great.*
—Mark Twain

Your friends are a powerful part of your hero's journey.
Really, they're the most important weapon in your
arsenal.

Every hero has his helpers. The Lone Ranger was, in fact,
not *alone*; he had Tonto. Luke had Han Solo. Frodo had Sam.
None of them would have gotten very far without help.

We've already discussed how important it is to build relationships. Developing your fan club is the natural evolution of this process.

Your fan club holds the key to everything that will make you successful. It will provide you with all of the tools you need. It's where the *real* magic happens. If you develop it fully, it can make you very powerful and very well known in your industry, and as a result, very successful in your business.

Thinking about your business relationships as a fan club helps you do the right things to maintain them. Don't think about it as a database, which makes it seem technical and cold. Actually think about it as a fan club, where there's love going both ways. Sure, there are different amounts of love, and different kinds, depending on who the fan is. But the bottom line is that there's a connection, a relationship that you nurture and maintain.

We all know how important it is to develop our network of contacts. Unfortunately, only a very small percentage of professionals build a fan club. That's where your opportunity lies.

Today, my core fan club is comprised of over five thousand people. When I first began it was zero.

I first started doing this when I was Magic Boy, and had a fan base that was unbelievably big. In reality, it was probably too big. At the time there wasn't the technology available today—yes, I'm old—but somehow I managed to track it all in a series of traditional address books. Each group had a separate address book, depending on the category. I'd write down each fan's name and all the information I could collect—contact details, spouse's name, kids' names and ages, when and where I met them, last time I had contact with them, etcetera. They were filled with hundreds of little sticky notes too. It was laughable. It was essentially a pre-historic version of what we call a CRM—customer relationship management—system today, but it paid big dividends. I rarely went without a gig.

Here's the good news. It's much easier today given the smartphones, software and other technology and systems we have at our disposal, so you don't have any excuses. Start small. Think big,

## Who are they?

They're the people that matter in the journey to your hero brand. Everyone from your clients and customers to your vendors and fellow trade association members.

Not everyone makes it into your fan club. It should only be the people you have a positive relationship with.

Let's start with the obvious. Your family should be in your fan club, as well as your team members. If they're not, something's gone terribly wrong.

Your family and your team members should be treated in a similar fashion, as far as your fan club is concerned. They are the people who will benefit most when things are good, and will likely be there to support you when things are bad. They're also the ones who will be affected most if things get tight. In short, they are the inside of your inner circle.

Your friends, your personal confidantes, should be added to the list as well.

Then come your clients, the people you do business with on a regular basis. Your customers want to know what you're doing. They want to be a part of your success, and they can provide you with referrals and references. In my world, my clients are often the first to know if someone's looking for a consultant. They will often say, "Let me introduce you."

Who else should be in your fan club? All of your key contacts in your trade associations. The movers and the shakers. The doers. Maintaining these relationships is vitally important to your positioning as an expert, for reasons already discussed.

Having key vendors in your fan club can have far-reaching benefits too. If you have a great relationship with them, they will know who you are and what you do, and occasionally recognize leads for you.

The rest of your fan club includes everyone else you interact with on a regular basis in your business life. Your media contacts are a must, as are prospects.

I also like to include people in other fields and industries, that *don't* do what I do, but that I have a connection with. They're excellent for bouncing ideas around, and they can often give you a fresh perspective or introduce you to new ideas. They could be people you meet in local organizations, or on a plane, or the friend of a friend.

If you've been maintaining all of these relationships on an ongoing basis, they will all know your "story," where you've been and where you're going.

Many people think there's an unlimited number of gifted and valuable people in the world, and they can always throw one away and go after the next. I strongly disagree. I have discovered there is not an unlimited number, and they all talk to each other. So, if you treat one poorly, or fail to maximize that relationship, you are doing a lot more damage to your personal brand and your business prospects than you realize.

That's your fan club in a nutshell: your family, team members, friends, clients, vendors, media contacts, and trade association contacts.

But now that you've got the list…

## How do you keep them?

It's simple. Keep them in the loop. Stay abreast of what they're doing, and let them know what you're up to. This has become a lot easier thanks to social media too.

Here's what I do. I keep my fan club list on my phone, and as I'm driving to Starbucks, or home from the airport, I'll pick out a few names on the list. Who haven't I talked to in a while? Then I'll just call out of the blue and I'll say, "What's up?" Initiate a conversation. "How are you? I saw on Facebook that you were in Italy with the wife and kids. How are things at work?"

It's all about staying in touch.

Here's an important tip: make sure you maintain those contacts when you *don't* need anything. Be a genuine *friend* and *fan.* You can't just call when you need something, because that will erode the relationship very quickly. If you've been calling all along, staying in touch, if and when you do need something, you're a lot more likely to get help.

And by all means, be there when they need you too. To have a friend, you need to be a friend. And don't forget to…

## Make new fans

Build the fan club process into everything you do. Whenever you're out, actively look around for potential new additions to your fan club.

For instance, when I finish a speech at an event, after the question-and-answer period, there's always a group of people waiting to talk to me. Most speakers experience this. But I will always stay until the last person is done talking to me. I'm never the guy who grabs his briefcase and heads for the door.

I'll talk to anyone who wants to talk to me, no matter how long it takes. I'll move to the side, or outside the door so I don't interfere with the next session or the clean up. I've had people stay for a long time, and generally they'll leave their business card. You can even suggest it and say, "Hey I'd like to stay in touch with you." Then I'll make some notes on the card—who they are and what they're about—and I'll stick it in my pocket. When I get back to my laptop, I'll add them to my fan club. They'll get the complete fan club treatment.

Despite what you were told in elementary school, whatever you do…

## Don't share

Your fan club is a private group. Do not share it with anybody, Guard it with your life. It takes a lot of work to create and maintain, and it's hard to place a dollar value on it. How valuable is it? It's…

## Prospecting gold

I use my fan club in my prospecting process. Once I've identified a potential client or opportunity, generally one of the first things I do is to call people within my fan club that may know the prospect, or background on the potential assignment. I'll say, "Hey, what do you know about this client, or potential hotel development?"

They'll give me the low-down *because* they're in my fan club. They want to see me succeed. Or sometimes they'll say, *don't* do it, and that's just as valuable because it saves me time and effort.

I do this *a lot*.

I'll call the vendors that may be doing business with that person or company. I'll ask them fifteen questions. What are they doing right now? Do you enjoy working with them? Are they financially strong? Have they had a lot of turnover? I'll ask about whatever I need to know, or I think might be important.

Sometimes I'll call other prospects in my fan club, people that I can't work with for one reason or another at the time, and say, "Hey this prospective client is in your neck of the woods. What can you tell me about her?"

The point is, by the time I finally walk into a meeting or hop on a call with that prospect, I'll probably already know if I have the business—or want it at least. I'll know a lot about the situation, and hopefully what the hot buttons or needs are. I'll know more about what to expect. I'm armed and ready.

When it's all finished, whether I get the business or not, I'll go back and thank the people in my fan club who helped me, and keep them up to date. "I met with this great lady, and you were right, she was everything you said." No matter how much time it takes to reach out to everybody that helped me, I'll do it. It's worth it.

That's how I keep my fan club. Everyone wants to be a part of the story. Everyone wants to know how it ends.

If I win the business, and there are certain people who helped me *win*, I'll make sure to thank and or reward them in a meaningful way. I guarantee you the next time an opportunity comes up, they'll help me again. Not just because they were rewarded. But because they feel respected, valued and appreciated.

And just to be clear, I would do the same for them any time.

## Exercise

1.  Create a database of your family, team members, friends, clients, professional colleagues, prospects, media contacts, and key vendors.
2.  Include all the information that you possibly can, name, address, phone numbers, e-mail addresses, birthdays, spouse or partner's names, names and ages of any children, alma mater, hobbies and other interests.
3.  Create a system to maintain contact on a regular basis. Be creative.

# 18

# MAKE-ME-FAMOUS CLIENTS

## Keep your eyes on the prize

> *If you have built castles in the air, your work*
> *need not be lost; that is where they should be.*
> *Now go put the foundations under them.*
> —Henry David Thoreau

> *The higher up you go, the more mistakes you're*
> *allowed. Right at the top, if you make enough*
> *of them, it's considered to be your style.*
> —Fred Astaire

Now that you've made the journey from invisible to icon, you're ready for the brass ring. You've climbed your way to expert standing in your category. Now you're ready to reap the rewards.

Now it's time to go after your *make-me-famous clients*.

These are the clients at the top of your industry. You probably can name a few right now, off the top of your head.

What does it take to be a make-me-famous client?

Well, by definition they have to be notable. They have to be recognized as the pinnacle by the power players in your industry. Sure, deep pockets are nice; they have to be able to pay their bills.

But to truly be a make me famous client, they need to give you the opportunity to do great work. They must give you the chance to do work that will get you noticed by everyone else in your field, work that will be remembered within your industry.

That's why they're called make-me-famous clients, after all.

## Every industry has them

It doesn't matter what business you're in. Whether you're an architect, an engineer, or a hotel, tourism and leisure consultant like me, you can find these golden clients in your field.

Sometimes it's simply one of the biggest names in your industry. Sometimes it's a company that's involved in an interesting, one-of-a-kind project. Sometimes it's a client that's revolutionizing the way things are done in their niche. But no matter what, it has to be a client that will let you do your best work.

Otherwise, it just won't help you get the notoriety you need for your hero brand.

For instance, if you're an architect or an engineer, an interior designer or a chef (or even a hotel guy), the Wynn Resort in Las Vegas would be an example of a make me famous client.

Why? Well, it's a landmark, for one thing. As of this writing, it's the largest five-star, five-diamond resort in Las Vegas. It receives continual coverage in the press—both trade and mainstream. Its founder, Steve Wynn, is a legend. Furthermore, when anyone walks through the doors of the Wynn, they're immediately impressed. Quality is reflected in every square inch, from the general architectural design to the décor to the bath fixtures. The guest service levels are also remarkably impressive.

So, if you are involved in a project with a client like that, the association with their name automatically strengthens your brand.

That's a make me famous client.

Early in my career, I had the privilege of landing a make me famous client. It was a company called Motorola. You may have heard of them.

Out of the blue, I found myself on the phone with a high-ranking officer from Motorola. She told me they were looking for some expertise in the hotel industry, because they were developing a new product for high-end resorts—a product that sold for over a million dollars. They needed someone who really understood the whole thought process from the hotel owner and manager's perspective. She said, "We've heard that you're an expert in this field." (You see what that expert tag can do?) Then she asked me if I would be willing to fly to their headquarters in Illinois to meet with them.

I said, "Well, of course I am." To make a long story short, after my presentation I ended up landing the business. To say it jumpstarted my consulting career would be an understatement.

The most beautiful part of it was that I didn't have to worry about the money. It was not an issue, so I was able to really focus on the quality of the strategy and the executions. It was some of the best work I'd ever done up to that time.

As a result, that work for Motorola won a slew of international awards. It opened doors for me that no amount of marketing or self-promotion ever could. Make-me-famous clients make the next client easy to get, and help you build your brand name as an expert.

Now, I have the privilege of working with make-me-famous clients every day—Marriott International, Hyatt Global,

IHG, BWH Hotels (Best Western Hotels & Resorts), and even Intel's IOT (Internet of Things) Group.

## Now it's your turn

Take a look at your industry. Who are the clients out there that could make *you* famous?

If you were a writer, for instance, Oprah would be a make me famous client. Can you imagine getting the chance to help her write her new autobiography? After that assignment, work would be pretty easy to come by.

Who are those clients in your industry? Remember, you're looking for clients that have recognizable names, pay their bills on time, let you do your best work, and have the potential to get you a lot of recognition for your *favorite* kind of work, for your *favorite* kind of client.

## How do you get one?

The truth is, most of the time make-me-famous clients have to come to you. They are generally challenging to reach. However, one of the best ways to land one is to become a recognized expert in your field, so they're more likely to seek you out. And you're already well on your way to meeting that goal.

But you can take steps to get closer. Begin by creating a list of 10-12 dream clients that you really want to work with. You can't do more than 12, and you really shouldn't have less, because you're dealing with long odds.

Once you have your list, learn everything you can about each of them and keep a file of your research.

When you've done your homework, reach out to decision makers within that dozen or so clients. Do everything in your power to add them to your fan club. When you meet one of those decision makers, you should be armed and ready to say "I know a lot about you and your company, and I'd like to work with you. I know that you just did X. I know that your company just did Y. I know you just bought Z. Any chance we could schedule a meeting to talk about how I, or my firm, can be of value to you?"

It can be a powerful pitch. You've demonstrated that you do your homework and are genuinely interested in them and their company. You're not asking for something from them, you're asking to contribute to whatever it is that they're doing.

If they don't agree to hand you the keys to the kingdom immediately, begin the old drip campaign—the constant contact. Don't be obnoxious. But every once in a while, send your decision maker something to remind them that you're out there, and that you're good at what you do. If it costs you dollars, make the investment based on that client's worth to you.

Start closing in on your make-me-famous clients. Do your homework. It's just a matter of time and effort.

That's how you get them. You'll win some, you'll lose some. If you run into someone who says absolutely no way for some reason, take them off your list. Then find someone else to put on the list, because there's always another one out there. Keep managing your list, and when you get some time, take your action steps.

It *will* pay off.

With a little luck, every once in a while you'll get a make me famous client just because you're a recognized expert in your field. They'll find *you*.

Just like they find me.

# 19

## NEVER STOP LEARNING

### The quest continues

> *Education is not the filling of a pail.*
> *It is the lighting of a fire.*
> —William Butler Yeats

> *Please sir, may I have some more?*
> —Oliver Twist (Charles Dickens)
> *The journey not the arrival matters.*
> —T. S. Eliot

Ultimately, being a known expert in an industry means you have knowledge and experience people value.

If you don't have that knowledge and experience, you're not an expert, you're just posing as one. And people will quickly learn the truth. They'll peek behind the curtain, and know you aren't really the wizard you claim to be. You'll be exposed.

It can happen in a number of ways.

If they're in the audience at a conference during one of your speeches or panel sessions, and they find you uninteresting, and leave feeling they learned nothing new or relevant, they may write you off. Then the next time you appear between the pages of a trade pub, or in an online piece, they'll flip or scroll past you. At the next conference, they may skip your session altogether. It could take a lot of time and effort to win them over again.

But that's not going to happen to you. You're not going to let it.

You're going to continue to build your knowledge as an expert. You're going to stay informed about what's going on in your world, in your industry. You're going to continue to explore all the forces that shape your profession and your niche. After all, you're passionate about all of these things anyway.

If you're a plumber and many of the plumbing supplies are made overseas, and there's a disaster looming at one of the big factories because of political unrest—or a pandemic—you need to foresee and communicate to others how it's going to impact your industry.

The truth is, if you're going to be successful in anything, you have to be perpetually learning. You need to continue to read books like this one. You must constantly strive to better yourself. You need to stay up on global and national news, and read your trade journals. You need to go online and continue to Google your important topics. You have to know who else is in your professional space, what they're saying, and whether you agree with them or not. You need to be familiar with the latest research in your industry, understand what the current trends are, and be able to make an educated guess what tomorrow's significant developments will be.

If you quit learning at any point, if you stop where you are and rest on your laurels, the guy across the street—or across the globe—will pass you up.

It's that simple. He'll have knowledge you don't. He'll be the recognized expert, not you.

Anything that's worth doing involves continually upgrading your knowledge as an expert.

My industry, hotels, is one of the oldest in the world, going back to when the inn was full the night Jesus was born. In many ways, it hasn't changed much. You still have a building filled with beds, and you still hope you'll see a friendly face when you arrive. Today, when a guest arrives at the Bellagio in Vegas, she checks in and goes to her room. The same thing happens every day at every hotel in the world, and it hasn't altered substantially for thousands of years.

The conversation today, however, is completely different than it was even three years ago. Post pandemic, the desired class of hotel and room décor has changed—think extended stay. The in-room amenities have become more focused on delivering against technology needs and green initiatives. The consumers' expectations regarding guest services are different. Even the industry's vocabulary is expanding to include ESG, DEI, AI, and other acronyms.

Every industry changes and you have to keep up with those changes. That's why you'll continue to read. That's why you'll continue to educate yourself. That's why you'll continue to go to the conferences.

You've arrived, and I'll bet you like it where you are. Now fight to stay there.

# 20

# *PROTECT YOUR BRAND*

## Check yourself

*Pride comes before a fall.*
—Proverb

*Success is not final, failure is not fatal: It is
the courage to continue that counts.*
—Winston Churchill

*Failure is simply the opportunity to begin
again, this time more intelligently.*
—Henry Ford

As we've discussed, your personal brand is your most valuable asset, representing your reputation, credibility, and the perception others have of you. It takes years of hard work, consistency, and careful decision-making to build a strong personal brand. However, it only takes a single misstep to damage it—sometimes irreparably. There are numerous real-life examples of celebrities who have tarnished their legacies due to poor choices and actions.

Once considered the epitome of golfing excellence and an inspiration to many, Tiger Woods' personal brand took a severe hit in 2009 when his extramarital affairs were exposed. The scandal shattered his clean-cut image, leading to a loss of endorsement deals, damaged personal relationships, and a tarnished reputation that still lingers today. Woods' actions demonstrated the importance of integrity, as even the most exceptional talent can be overshadowed by personal misconduct.

Bill Cosby, once hailed as "America's Dad" and a respected figure in the entertainment industry, saw his personal brand crumble when numerous women accused him of sexual assault. The allegations shattered the image he had cultivated over decades, leading to criminal charges, public backlash, and the cancellation of his projects. Cosby's downfall underscores the significance of authenticity and the devastating consequences of betraying public trust.

Lance Armstrong was a cycling legend and an inspiration to millions, having conquered cancer and won the Tour de France a record seven times. However, his personal brand took a near fatal crash when he admitted to doping throughout his career. Armstrong's confession not only led to the stripping of his titles and sponsorships but also eroded the faith of his fans and damaged his reputation irreparably. This example emphasizes the importance of honesty and transparency in maintaining a strong personal brand.

The list of examples is seemingly endless.

Lindsay Lohan, the former child star who struggled with legal issues, substance abuse, and erratic behavior, negatively impacting her reputation.

Mel Gibson, the renowned actor and director who faced public backlash after making controversial and offensive remarks.

Paula Deen, the celebrity chef who faced backlash and lost endorsement deals after admitting to using racial slurs.

Kanye West, the rapper and fashion designer who faced criticism for controversial statements, social media outbursts, and erratic behavior—literally lost his billionaire status overnight.

Will Smith, the former rapper and mega action movie star who has been living with the repercussions of his infamous Oscars slap for two years now.

You get the idea, and I'm certain you can come up with your own list of celebrities, c-suite executives, and perhaps even co-workers, friends and family who have significantly damaged their personal brands through poor decision making.

That's why it's so important today that you make every effort to...

## Protect your brand

To avoid the fate suffered by these celebrities, it's essential to be mindful of your decision making and actions. Here are some key principles to protect and enhance your personal brand:

> **Authenticity** – always remain true to yourself and maintain consistency between your public image and personal values.
>
> **Integrity** – uphold moral and ethical standards, and act in ways that align with your personal brand.

**Responsibility** – take ownership of your actions and be accountable for their consequences.

**Thoughtful Engagement** – be very mindful of your online presence and interactions, as they can impact your personal brand significantly.

**Continuous Improvement** – invest in personal growth, develop new skills, and evolve to stay relevant and authentic.

Building a strong personal brand is a valuable asset, but it can be easily tarnished by a single misstep. The cautionary tales of celebrities like Tiger Woods, Bill Cosby, and Lance Armstrong remind us of the importance of upholding integrity, authenticity, and responsibility.

The lesson is that you must...

## Think, and be aware

Thinking before you act, speak, write, pose or post is key. Ensure that *everything* you do, say, write and or post is entirely consistent with your personal brand and values, as it will most likely be in the public domain instantaneously—and remain there forever.

Be keenly aware of your environment. Today, you should assume that no matter where you find yourself, you're most likely being recorded—often without notice or permission—due to advancements in technology. Think personal devices, security focused surveillance in public spaces, and perhaps even intelligent virtual assistants like "Alexa."

When at conferences, and other business or social events, you should be mindful of your behavior, who you are mingling with or posing for pictures next to, and how it may look to others through the lens. Unprofessional actions and controversial affiliations may have long-lasting consequences on your personal brand and professional opportunities.

By being highly conscious of your actions, you can manage and protect your reputation effectively. However, if something negative should occur, remember that it may not be...

## The end of the world

Strong personal brands can often be repaired. There are also many examples of celebrities who have successfully overcome damage to their personal brands.

Robert Downey Jr. faced a period of personal struggles and legal issues related to substance abuse in the late 1990s and early 2000s. However, he made a remarkable comeback and rebuilt his career, becoming one of the most bankable and beloved actors of his generation, particularly through his portrayal of Iron Man in the Marvel Cinematic Universe, and as Sherlock Holmes in the highly successful Guy Ritchie-directed series of films.

Martha Stewart, the renowned businesswoman and television personality I held up as an example earlier in the book, faced a setback when she was convicted and imprisoned for insider trading in 2004. However, she successfully rebuilt her brand after her release from prison, re-establishing herself as a lifestyle expert and continuing her successful ventures in cooking, home decor, and media.

Even Tiger Woods made a remarkable comeback in his career, winning multiple tournaments and regaining his status as one of the top golfers in the world.

In truth, everyone loves a comeback story. So don't assume a ding to your personal brand will take you out of the game. Just be apologetic, transparent, remind your audience of your values, and do your best to return to the *right path* of your personal brand journey.

By understanding the power of personal branding and pro-actively safeguarding your reputation, you can navigate the public sphere with care and protect your legacy for years to come.

# 21

CHAPTER

# A PIVOTAL DECISION

## From lifestyle to legacy

> *Life isn't about finding yourself. Life*
> *is about creating yourself.*
> —George Bernard Shaw

> *There are three classes of people: those who see, those*
> *who see when they are shown, those who do not see.*
> —Leonardo da Vinci

> *The secret of change is to focus all of your energy, not*
> *on fighting the old, but on building the new.*
> —Socrates

As a successful solo practitioner, working under the John Fareed Hospitality Consulting brand, I had the freedom and flexibility to shape my own path. One that supported my desired lifestyle and fulfilled my immediate needs. I had the autonomy to choose my clients and projects, and to determine when and how much I wanted to work. Most importantly, I enjoyed a fairly decent income.

My boutique, low-overhead firm provided a healthy work-life balance for me personally, one that prioritized flexibility and time off over business growth or expansion. In short, I was nearly living Tim Ferriss's fabled *4-Hour Workweek.*

## Then I experienced an awakening

Turns out, my successful lifestyle firm was essentially worthless, and held no real value. I came to this conclusion based solely upon observation.

I witnessed a number of solo practitioners in my industry—including many of my friends and mentors in the International Society of Hospitality Consultants—exit their well-known firms with little more than the personal income and assets they had managed to set aside. There was no "liquidity event," or "big pay day," from the sale of their practices upon retirement.

It became evident to me that a business solely reliant on the owner's involvement for its success—like mine—holds little value when the principal exits.

Despite the success and fulfillment I experienced as a solo practitioner, this was a rude awakening.

After this epiphany, I vowed to...

## Make a pivot

This *awakening* was the primary motivation behind my pivot from a solo practitioner, boutique firm, that provided a comfortable lifestyle, to one designed to create an enduring asset for future opportunities and an eventual exit.

I believed that transitioning from a lifestyle business to an asset-focused one would allow for the cultivation of a robust foundation, enabling long-term growth and attracting potential partners, successors or investors—who might buy me out at some point.

I believe the strategic shift will allow me to maximize the potential return on investment when the time for my retirement approaches. We'll see how it unfolds, but I still feel it was my best bet strategically.

## Embarking on a new path

After I made my decision, I began mapping out the crossroads and hidden paths to the next destination on my journey. I spent the next several months seeking navigational advice from business experts like John Warrillow, author of *Built to Sell* and *The Art of Selling Your Business*; Mark Tepper author of *Walk Away Wealthy*; and Kevin Short, author of *Sell Your Business for An Outrageous Price*.

I searched for and consumed relevant articles in *Inc.*— Norm Brodsky's column was highly insightful—*Fast Company* and *Entrepreneur* magazines.

However, I garnered the most valuable advice from others who had successfully navigated the journey, including fellow industry colleagues who had transformed their practices and experienced the "big pay day." I reached out to a number of them, shared my story, and asked if they'd be generous enough to take the time to speak with me about their journeys (over an expensive lunch or dinner of course). Several took me up on the offer. They shared amazingly similar stories about overcoming inner demons and self-doubt, dangers and pitfalls, and ultimately emerging triumphant. For a few thousand dollars spent on airfare, hotels, food and adult beverages, I experienced a master class in entrepreneurship.

I learned that transitioning to an asset-focused business model involved implementing robust systems, processes, and a competent management team that reduces my day-to-day involvement.

Why is this important?

Because I also learned that I can no longer be synonymous with the company. I had to find a way to relieve my firm's moniker of John Fareed. If potential partners, investors or buyers weren't confident that the business could run without me, I might never enjoy a "liquidity event."

More importantly, by diversifying the business, and reducing its reliance on a single individual—me—the risks associated with unforeseen circumstances, such as health issues or burnout, were mitigated.

Essentially, a well-structured and independent business has greater appeal to potential buyers or successors, further reducing risk and increasing the perceived value.

I have to admit, the thought of shelving my name and well-known rhino logo was more traumatic than I can express here, but I knew I had to trust the new direction I *needed* to embark upon.

Once again, I found myself ready to…

## Take a leap

I spent the next month researching options, starting with a list of competitive firms that I felt I could possibly acquire, or with whom I could merge. I found none of the options particularly appealing, or practical.

I also looked at several independent member firm networks focused on the hotel industry. Much like Deloitte, KPMG and

PwC, reputable independent member firm networks generally offer numerous advantages, including a recognized global brand and footprint; access to important resources such as operational systems and tools, marketing support, and training; business referrals; knowledge sharing; and instant industry credibility and reputation.

I came to understand that the process of becoming a member firm is no easy feat. First and foremost, the geographic opportunity has to be open and available. Second, applicants must possess a strong P&L and balance sheet, and a demonstrative track record of high business standards and ethics. Once submitted the application must work its way through an approval process, usually conducted by a committee or board of directors. The process can take three to six months.

After much due diligence, I felt this was my best path forward. I opted to pursue Horwath HTL. James Chappell, global business director, had attempted to recruit me a few times, and was surprised and pleased to learn that I was finally ready to take the leap and fully commit to the network—assuming they would have me of course.

The allure of becoming part of a globally recognized network of consulting firms, known for its industry expertise and leadership, proved difficult to resist. The prospect of collaborating with renowned professionals, accessing an extensive network of resources, and exposure to a wider range of projects and clients excited me. I saw this as an opportunity to expand my horizons and take my business life to new heights.

A few weeks later, I flew to London to meet with James face-to-face and began the application process—fully leveraging my personal brand, industry experience and accolades to their highest value. A couple of months later, I was proud and honored to receive a call from James and heard him say the life changing words...

## Welcome to Horwath HTL

Joining the Horwath HTL network allowed me to instantly tap into the global reputation and industry leadership built over its 100-plus years, further positioning me as a trusted authority in hotel, tourism, and leisure consulting. It also greatly expanded my professional network.

As a result, my personal brand gained a significant boost, which in turn attracted high-profile clients, challenging projects, and other lucrative opportunities that I wouldn't have had otherwise.

During my first five years with the network, I navigated a path from managing director of the Orlando, Florida office, to chairman of North America, to global chairman. It's been an amazing journey thus far.

I've gained invaluable knowledge and experience which has enhanced my professional skill set. The global reach of the firm has provided opportunities to work on projects across diverse geographies and cultures. In addition, it has broadened my perspective and deepened my understanding of the industry's complexities.

The pivot has forever altered...

## Everything, including my future

The exposure to a multitude of projects, combined with the guidance and mentorship of my colleagues in the network, has undoubtedly created a solid foundation for future growth.

The decision was not without its challenges, but the rewards on this new path have already made it a worthwhile endeavor. Ultimately, this shift allowed me to forge a more fulfilling and prosperous future, while creating a solid foundation for long-term success.

The transition from a lifestyle business to an asset-focused enterprise represented a significant shift in mindset. However, embracing the idea of creating a valuable asset that can be sold or passed on as a legacy, transformed my firm into something that will transcend my own personal needs.

The transition may also allow for the creation of generational wealth, enabling me to pass down the business to family members, partners or future entrepreneurs, ensuring a lasting impact beyond my tenure.

Finally, this strategic approach may allow me to exit on my own terms, ensuring a smooth transition, while maximizing the financial rewards of my years of dedication and hard work, and securing the financial future I'd hoped for all along.

Best of all...

## I *still* have a good lifestyle

Turns out, I didn't have to sacrifice as much as I thought I would either. Being global chairman is a huge responsibility, but it provides a very good lifestyle.

My weeks are always different.

I travel a lot internationally for strategic meetings, recruitment efforts, and speaking engagements, all of which I genuinely enjoy.

Whenever possible, I also visit our member offices around the globe to interact with them, their teams and key clients. It's my way of inspiring and motivating our members by demonstrating my commitment and love of the Horwath HTL brand. I feel so very privileged to be working with our amazing colleagues around the world.

I've also maintained a great deal of autonomy, and I still enjoy a fairly decent income.

Most importantly however, I now have...

## Proof of concept

As I shared earlier, the pandemic negatively affected the hotel, tourism and leisure industry more than most others.

Remember, years ago it was the economic crisis caused by the after-effects of 9/11 that effectively put an end to my hotel marketing firm, and spurred me to write *From Invisible to Icon* in the first place.

This time, however, the power of my personal brand helped me not just push through the pandemic, but thrive.

In other words, my approach worked.

My multi-year plan to reposition my personal brand away from *hotel marketing expert* to that of a highly recognized, well-educated and experienced full-service industry consultant was successful. All of the time, energy and money spent pursuing the right skills, the right credentials, and the right education, paid off—big time.

Throughout the crisis, my consulting and advisory services were in high demand. Hotel owners, investors, lenders, management companies, and global brands all sought my insights, solutions, and guidance towards forging a path forward.

Ultimately, making the pivot from a lifestyle business to an asset-focused one, was the best decision of my professional life.

# FINAL THOUGHT

## The cowboy boots story

*Opportunities multiply as they are seized.*
—Sun Tzu

*Opportunities are like sunrises. If you
wait too long, you miss them.*
—William Arthur Ward

*If a window of opportunity appears,
don't pull down the shade.*
—Tom Peters

As you know by now, before I was the *Consulting Guy*,
I was *Magic Boy*. For the better part of fifteen years,
I performed magic professionally aboard cruise ships,
in casinos, and at private clubs around the world including the
famed Magic Castle in Hollywood, California.

So, do you want to read about the greatest magic trick I
ever performed?

Yes?... Thanks for playing along.

It was Christmas Eve, the best night of the year to perform on a cruise ship—or anywhere for that matter. I was in the
middle of my show, finishing up a rope trick, when I noticed a

little boy seated in the front row who had obviously opened his Christmas presents already.

He was six or seven years old, wearing a black cowboy hat—with the red wooden bead on the chin string cinched tight under his nose—a cowhide vest, a couple of six shooters strapped to his waste by a Texas size buckled belt , and Levi's tucked into a brand new pair of shiny cowboy boots.

But something wasn't right. I caught myself laughing as I realized that he wasn't quite tall enough for his feet to touch the floor, and his boots were obviously too big for his feet. Funnier still, his shiny new boots were on the wrong feet!

As he sat there, making a little semi circle with his boots, I fought back the laughter and asked the question every magician asks at some point in his show, "Who would like to help me with the next trick?"

The young cowboy sprang to his feet, waved his hand in the air and shouted, "Hey pick me mister. Pick me!" What could I do? I said, "Sure come on up."

After the introductions and thanking him for volunteering, I grabbed his shoulders as if repositioning him on stage and said, "Stand right here over the trap door." I got down on one knee and asked all the usual questions I ask first graders, "So, are you married?"—you'd be surprised how many say yes and point to their mom or dad.

I started to comment on the shiny new boots when suddenly it dawned on me. I looked down at the boy and said, "This is going to blow your mind… SHAZAM! Your boots have changed feet!"—insert visual of overly dramatic *magical* flourish here.

The boy glanced down at his feet and threw the audience a perfect "shock and awe" face. Then he quickly sat down, pulled his boots off, put them on the right feet, ran off the stage and hid behind his mother.

The audience roared with laughter. I realized immediately that it would be the best magic trick I would ever perform.

Despite the fact that they may have had a drink or two, the audience figured out what had happened, and felt as though they were in on the joke. For the rest of the week, the boy was the star of the cruise. Passengers would call him over and say, "How did that magician make your boots change feet?" The frustrated boy would reply, "I don't know! He won't tell me!"

It was perfect. The little boy and his family had a unique story to tell when they got home—as did all the passengers—and I had won their collective affection with something so simple, yet unrepeatable.

Had I gone on to perform the usual trick from my repertoire, the show would have been good, but it wouldn't have had that warm and fuzzy moment. Had I not noticed the boots and thought of a way to take advantage of them, we would have all missed that special "shared" moment—that emotional connection.

I guess that's the point of my story. The secret to success is learning to recognize opportunities, no matter how small, and identifying ways in which to take advantage of them.

Hopefully, you found this book full of opportunities. Ones that you want to take advantage of as you begin crafting a personal brand that lifts you up, pushes you forward and helps you accomplish all that you dare to dream.

You can do it. Whatever it is. Don't let anyone tell you otherwise. Just flex that chutzpah muscle and go for it. The journey to *your* hero brand awaits.

# ACKNOWLEDGMENTS

First, I would like to express my sincere gratitude to Sean Hunter for being my co-pilot on *this* hero's journey—again.

I especially want to thank my friend and *factotum*, Helen Nadon, for her encouragement and assistance, and more importantly, for serving as editor in chief on both the first and this revised and expanded edition.

My friend Tom "Spike" Macaluso for the cover design and layout. Thank you for being so generous with your time and creativity.

Thanks go to James Chappell too for penning the book's foreword.

Finally, I would like to thank most sincerely my late mother Mervette, who instilled in me a belief that I can accomplish anything I dare to dream.

# ABOUT JOHN FAREED

John Fareed is a personal branding and performance coach, a highly sought-after keynote speaker, and author of *From Invisible To Icon—How To Become A Known Expert In Your Industry*.

Fareed is global chairman of Horwath HTL, the global leader in hotel, tourism, and leisure consulting. The hundred-year-old firm boasts 250 senior consultants working out of sixty offices in more than fifty countries.

He has spoken at industry events in Australia, Brazil, Croatia, Egypt, France, Germany, Hungary, Ireland, Italy, Mexico, Oman, United Kingdom, United Arab Emirates, and across the US, Canada and Caribbean.

National television programs including ABC News, CNN and Fox News Network have used Fareed as their industry authority and his expert opinions can be found in publications such as the New York Times, USA Today, and the Wall Street Journal.

Fareed holds two postgraduates including a Master of Science degree from the Dublin Institute of Technology's, currently Technological University Dublin, School of Hospitality Management and Tourism in Dublin, Ireland as well as a Hotel Real Estate Investments and Asset Management Certificate from Cornell University. He holds professional designations from the prestigious International Society of Hospitality Consultants (ISHC) and the Hospitality Sales and Marketing Association International (HSMAI). HSMAI recognized Fareed as one of the "Top 25 Extraordinary Minds in Sales and Marketing." He is Chair Emeritus of both ISHC and the Board of Trustees for HSMAI's International Foundation.

Prior to his distinguished consulting career, Fareed spent fifteen years as a professional magician performing on cruise ships, in casinos and at private clubs such as the famed Magic Castle in Hollywood, California. He also served six years in the US Marine Corps. In his mid-thirties, Fareed began a successful, hotel, tourism and leisure consulting career as a solo practitioner, having never worked in the industry—and without the benefit of a college education. He spent the next thirty years advancing from "invisible to icon" in the industry.

No matter your age, education, or where you are in your career, John Fareed can help you become an icon in your industry too. Why not begin the journey today? To learn more, or to book a keynote or workshop, reach out via jf@johnfareed.com.

# ABOUT SEAN HUNTER

Sean Hunter grew up in the Florida hospitality industry as Orlando rose from a small town of orange groves to a premier travel destination. As a child, he saw people from all around the world on vacation and witnessed what their adventures meant to them, sparking a life-long fascination with travel.

A writer all his life, Sean's work is a synthesis of his love of travel and his love of story, and he continues to explore new creative possibilities.

His wanderlust has led him to embark on many memorable cross-country trips with his own family, visiting 48 of the 50 States with his wife and four boys. He's lived in Florida, California, New Mexico, and currently resides in Japan, as he continues his quest to explore the frontier where travel meets personal narrative. He is currently mapping out his next adventure.